THIS BOOK BELONGS TO:

_____

About Whyte Canvas LLC

Whyte Canvas Books is a small owned business that specializes in unique coloring books. Each page is lovingly crafted, offering a canvas for creativity to flourish. Whether you're a child discovering the joy of coloring or an adult seeking relaxation, our books provide a unique outlet for expression. With every stroke of color, our pages come alive, inviting you into a world of imagination and artistry.

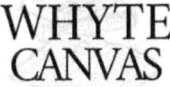

If you are using markers, we recommend putting a protective sheet behind the page you are coloring!

WHYTE CANVAS

Copyright © 2024 Whyte Canvas LLC

Unauthorized reproduction, distribution, or usage of any images or designs contained herein is strictly prohibited without prior written consent except for brief quotations in critical reviews and other specific noncommercial uses. Purchasing this coloring book grants you the non-exclusive, non-transferable right to use the images for personal enjoyment and coloring purposes only. Any commercial or derivative use of these images without express permission is prohibited. Thank you for respecting the creativity and hard work that went into making this coloring book a reality.
ALL RIGHTS RESERVED

Thank you for choosing our coloring book!

Your support means the world to us. We hope you enjoy the intricate designs and joyful creativity within these pages. Your feedback is invaluable to us, so if you loved your experience with our book, we would greatly appreciate it if you could take a moment to leave an honest review on Amazon. Your thoughts will help others discover the joy of coloring and encourage us to keep creating beautiful content. For more captivating designs and updates,

visit us at
www.whytecanvasbooks.com
Happy coloring!

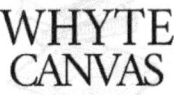

Color Test Page

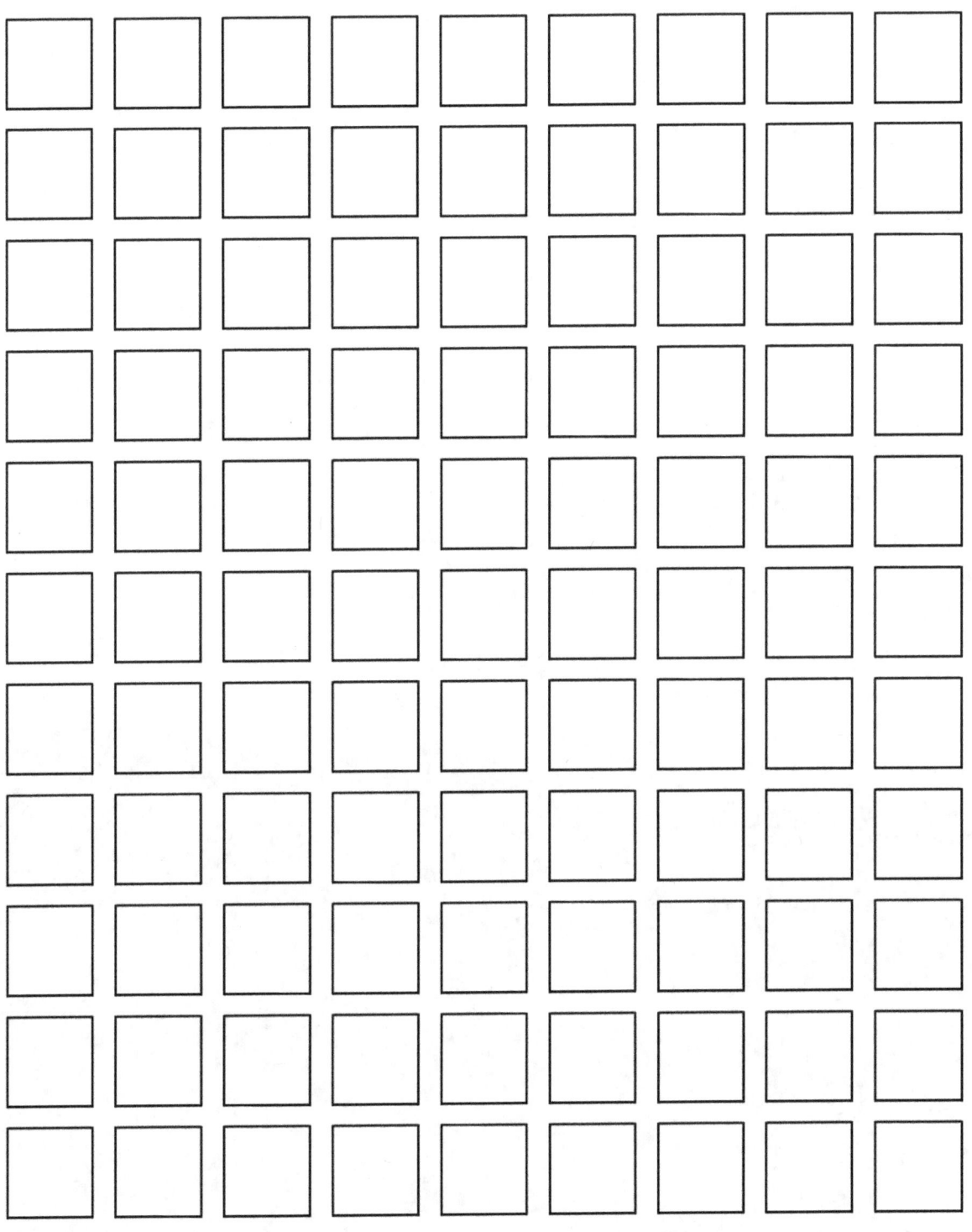

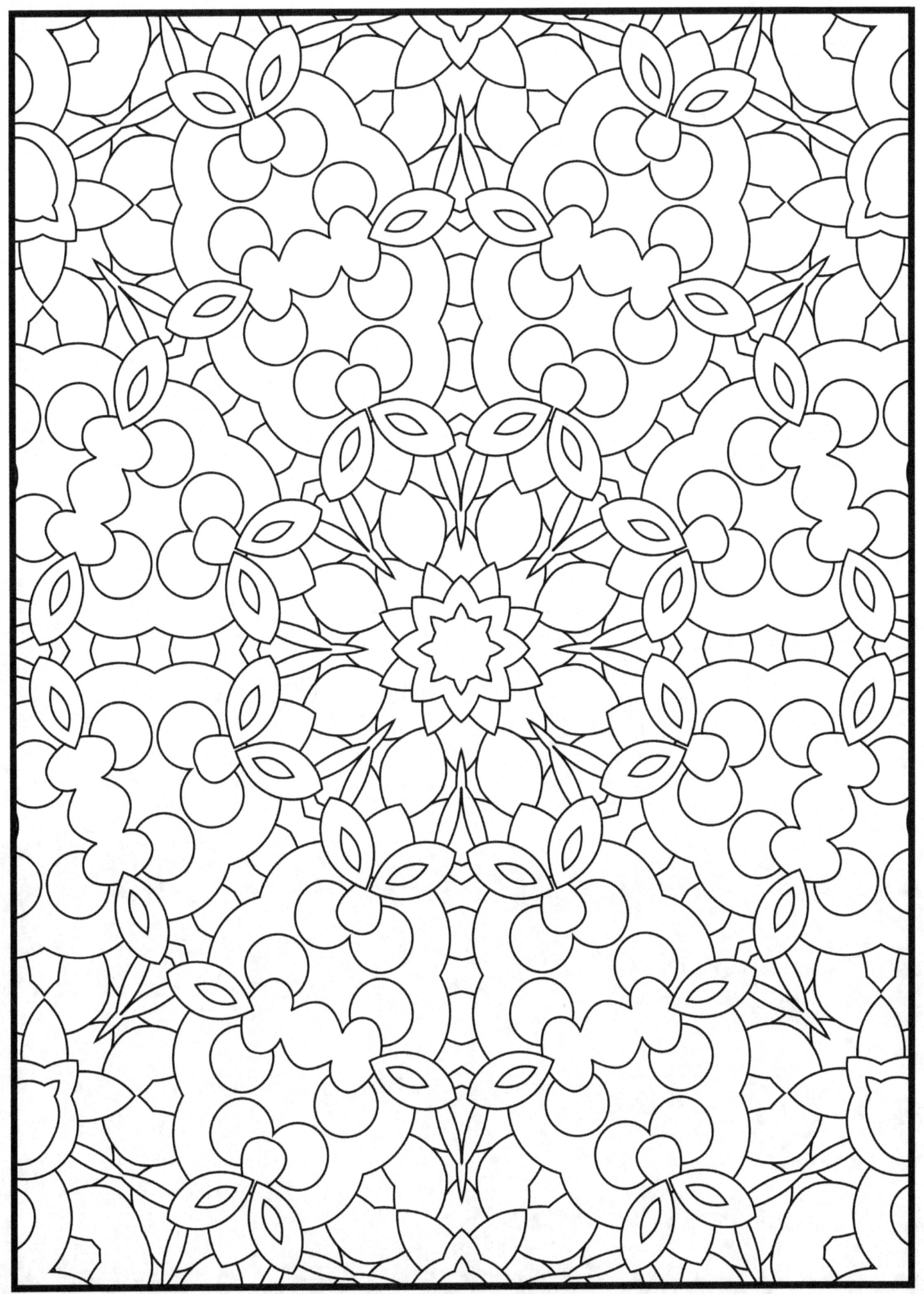

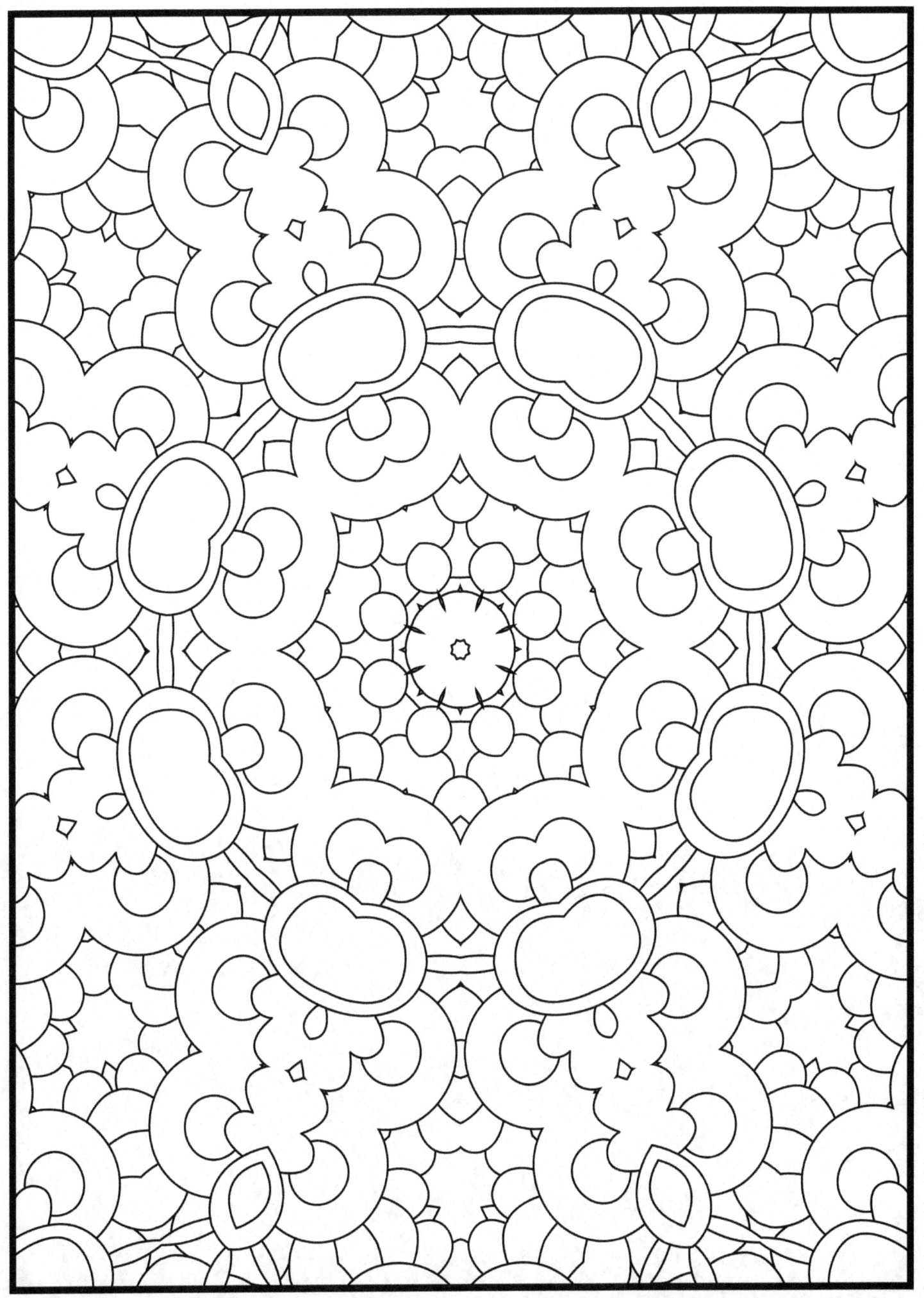

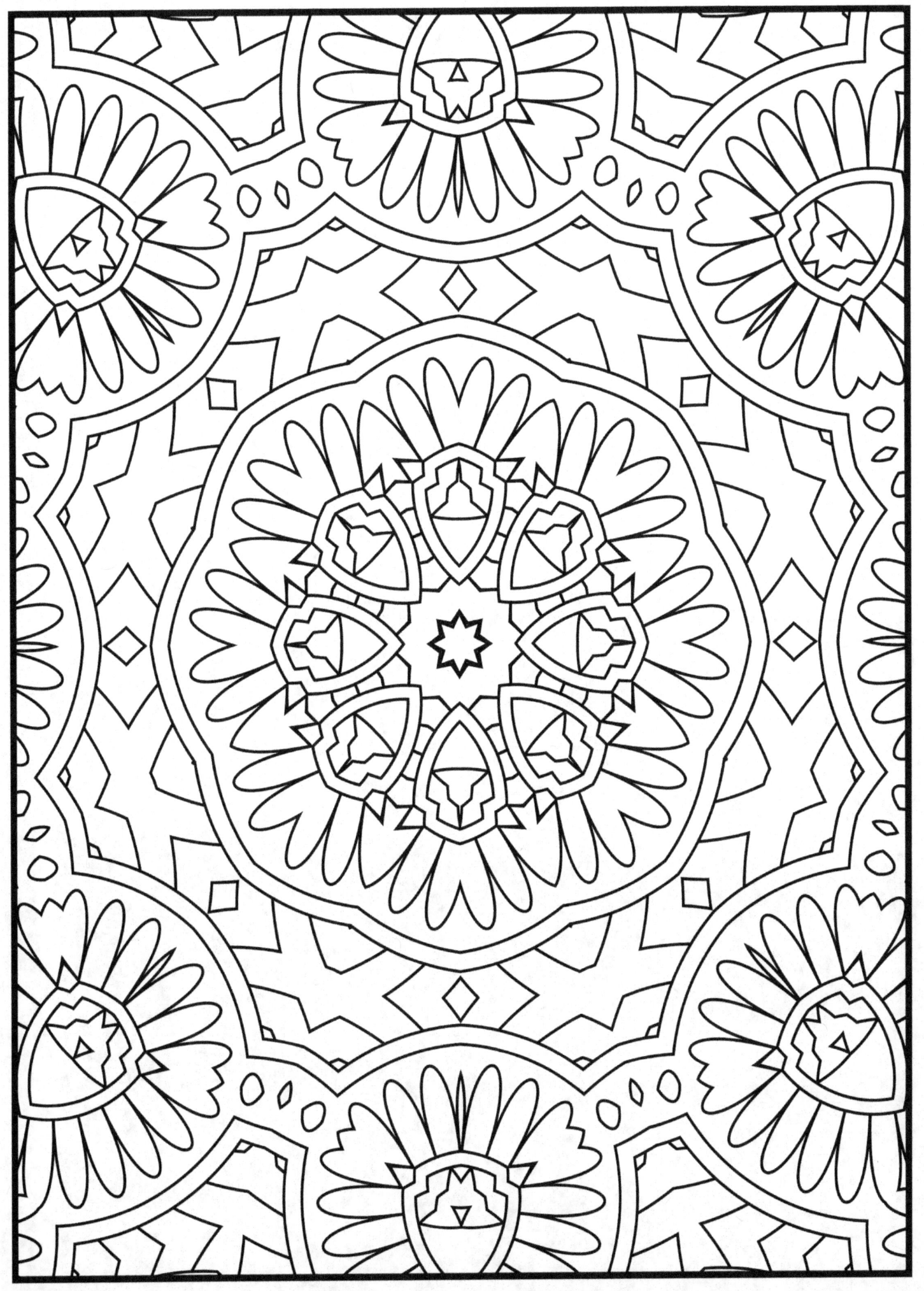

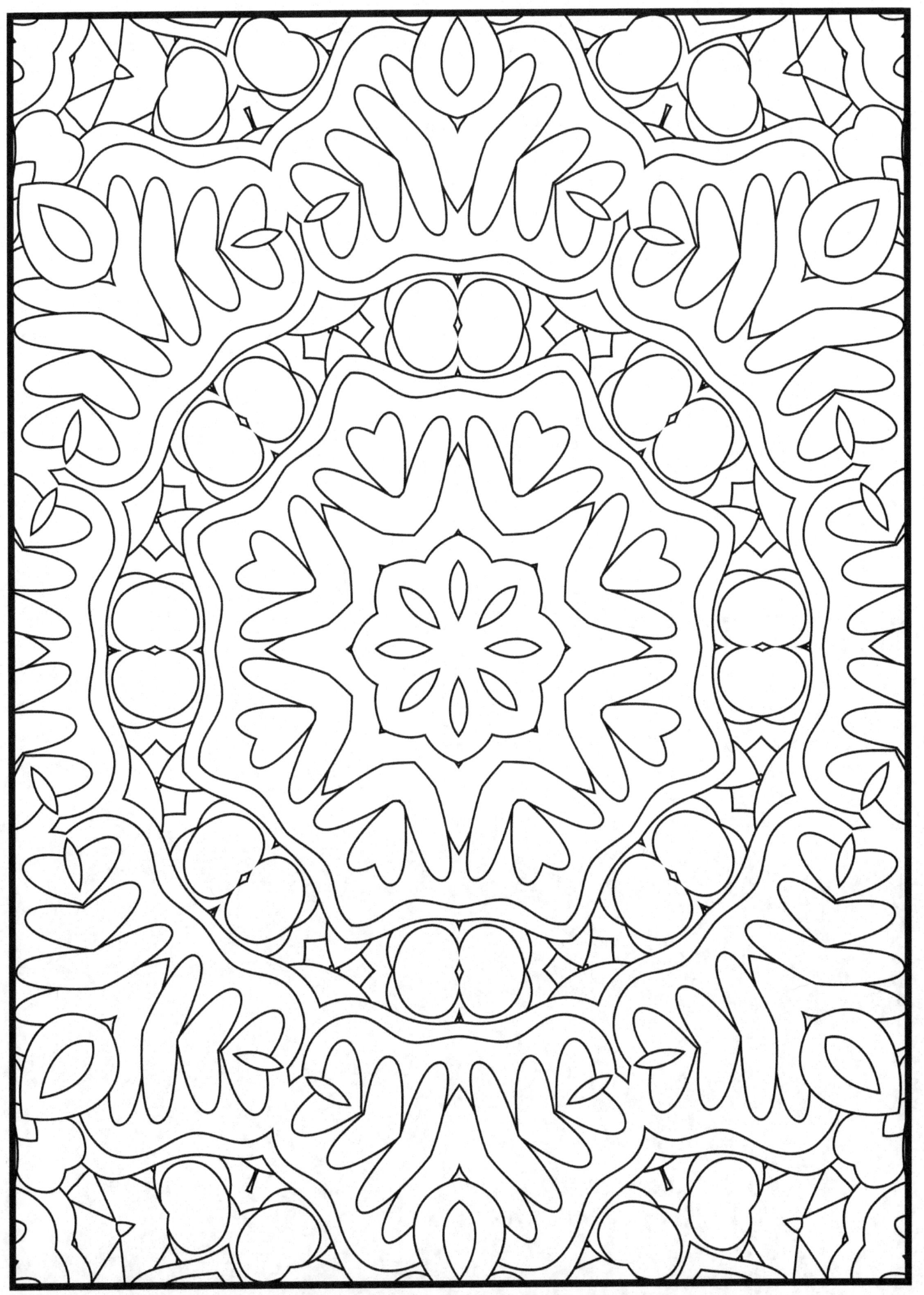

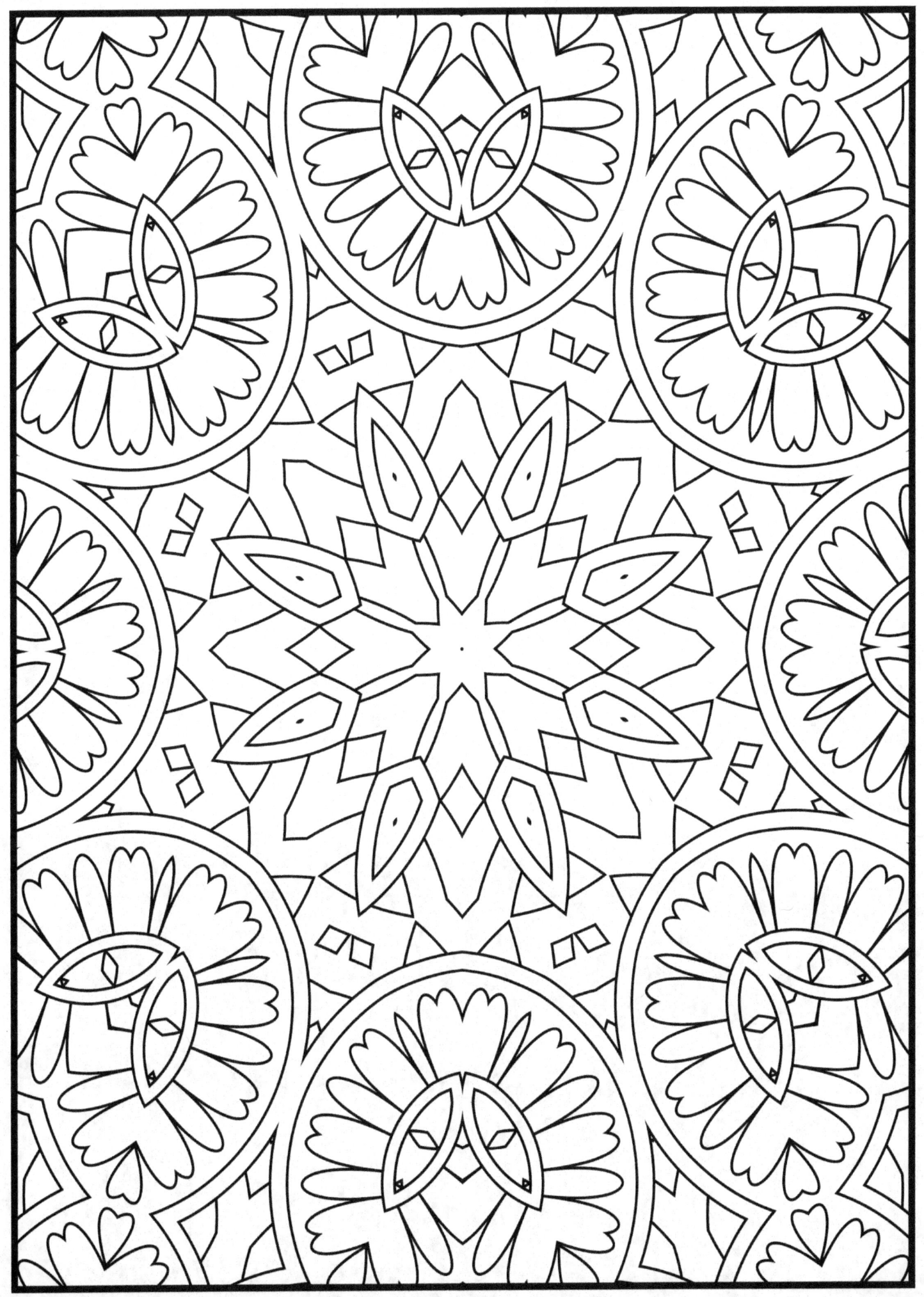

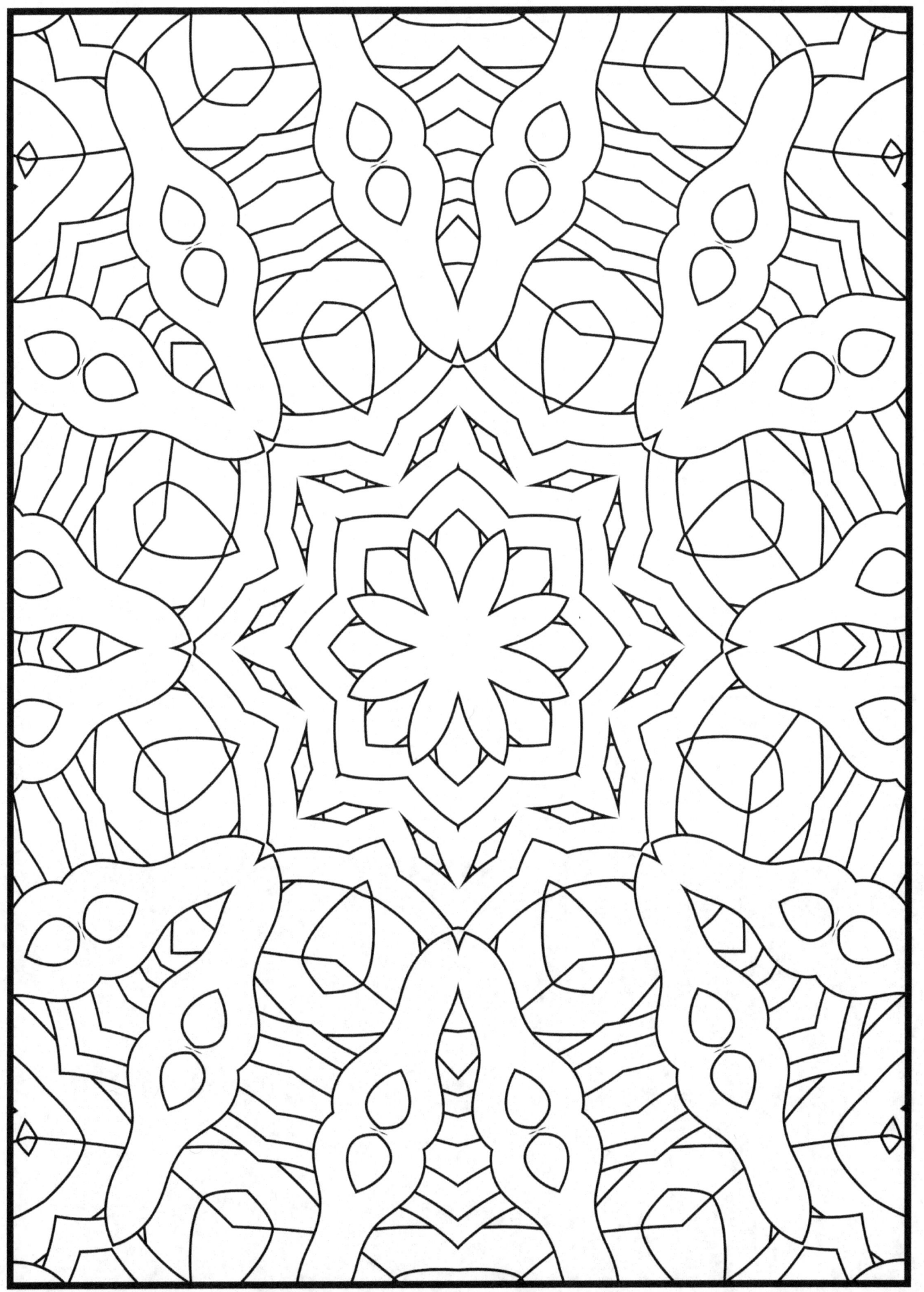

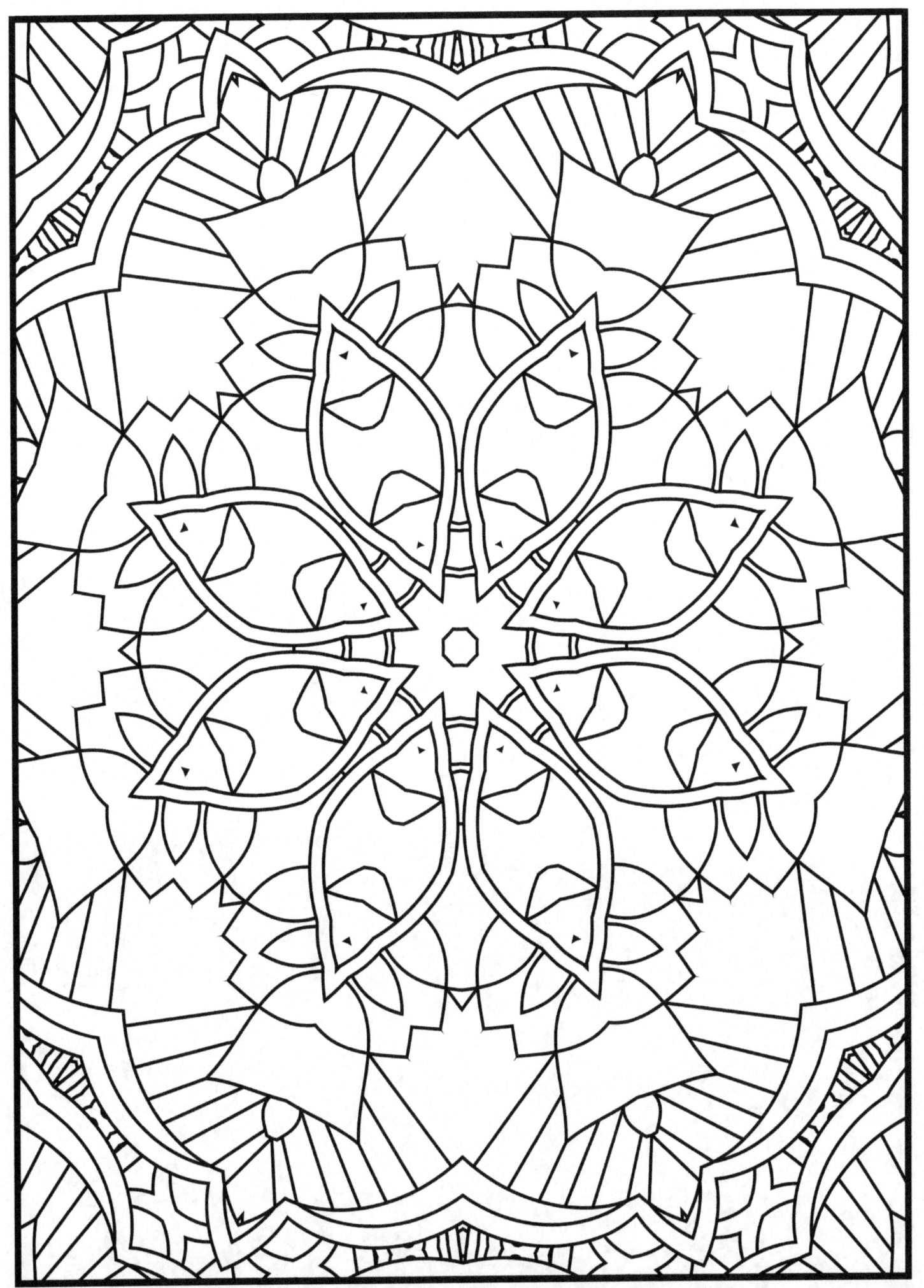

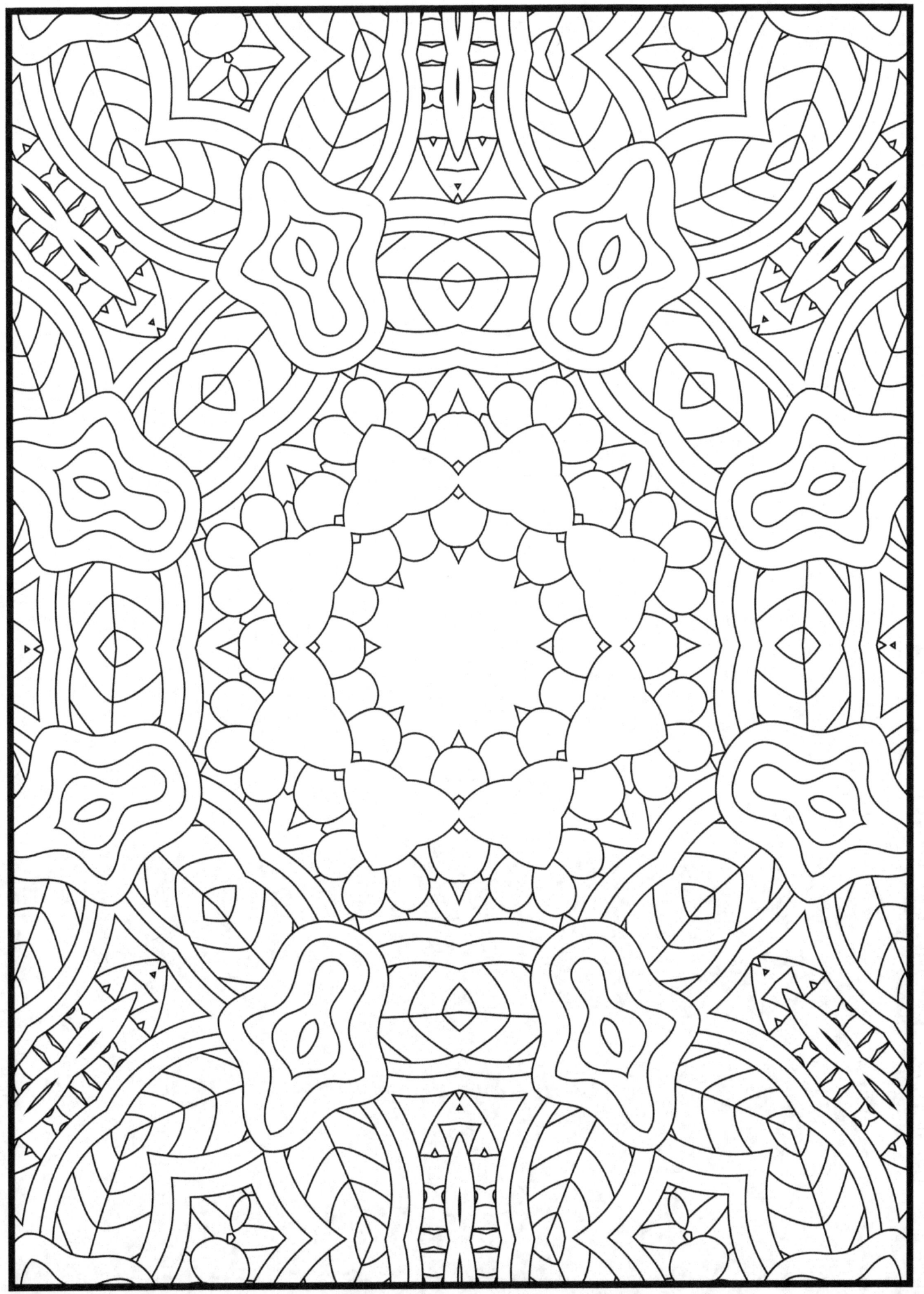

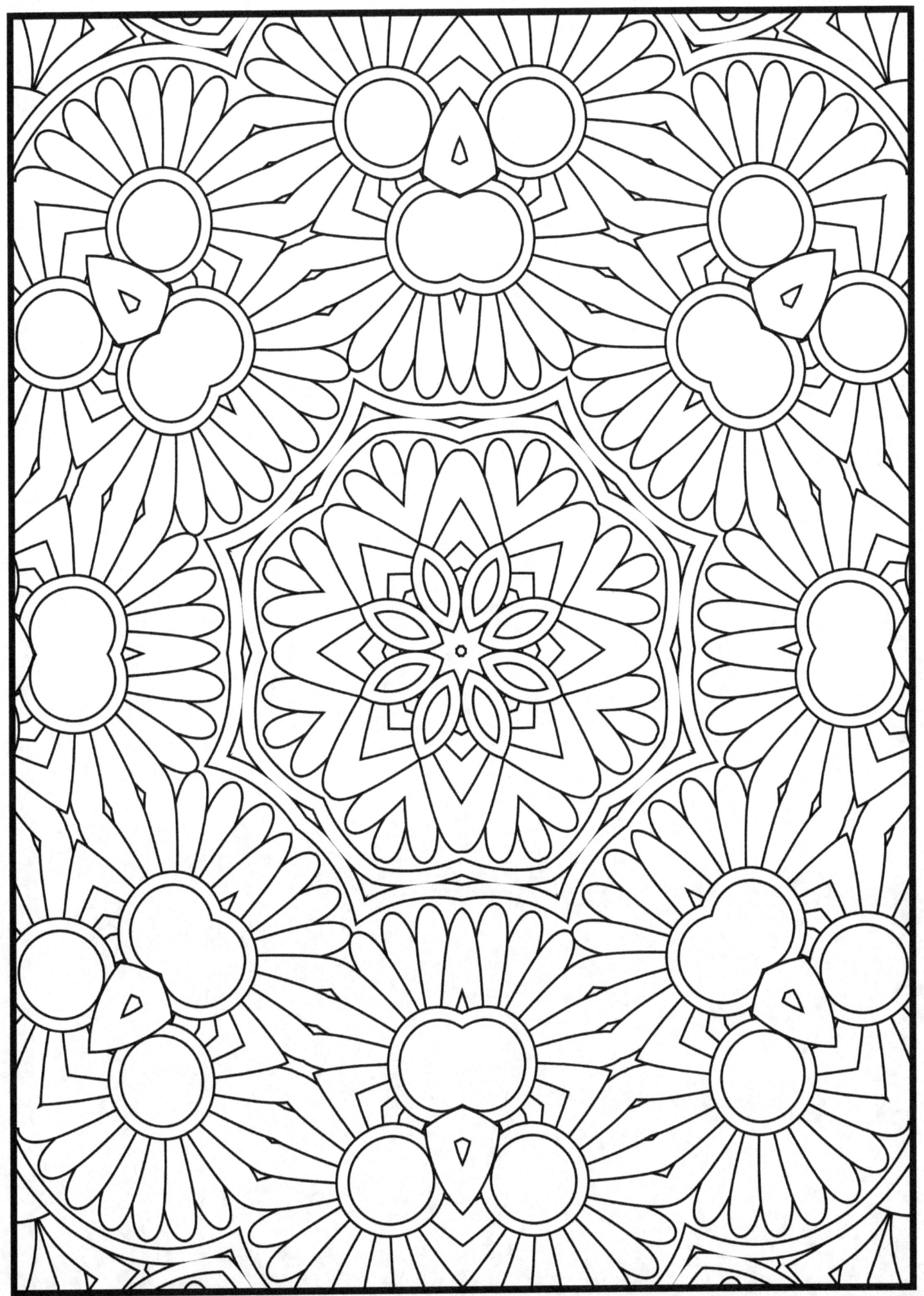

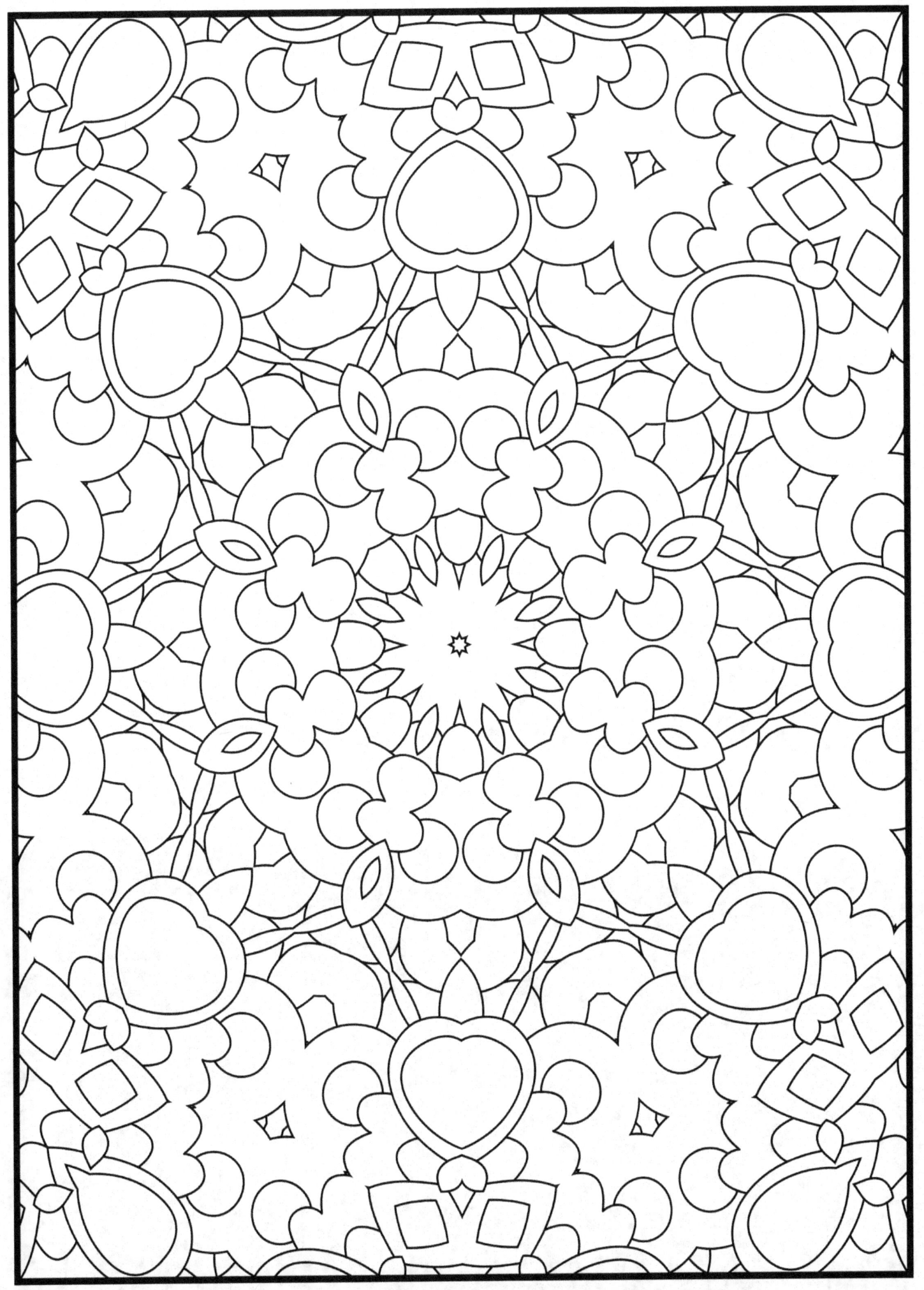

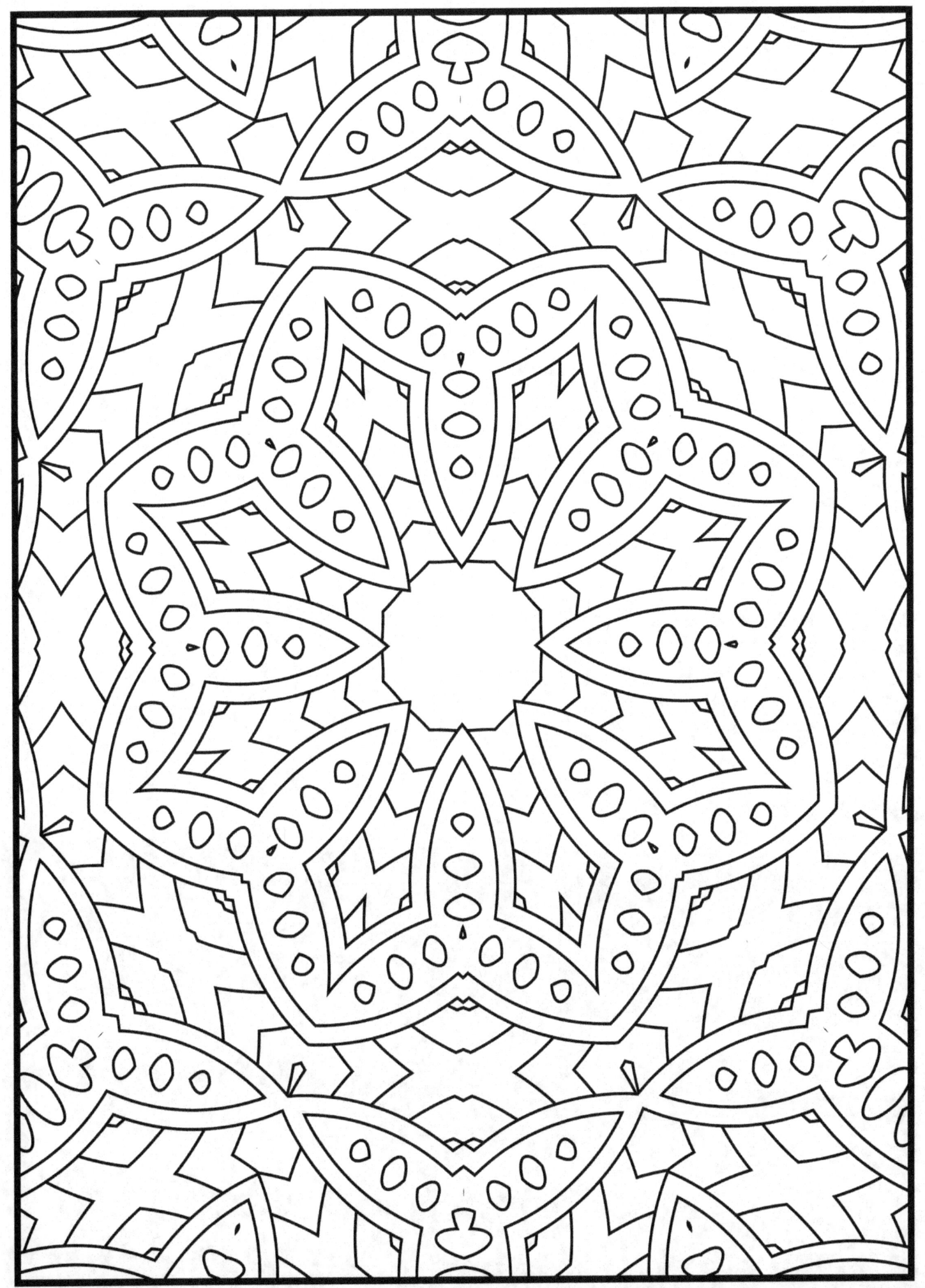

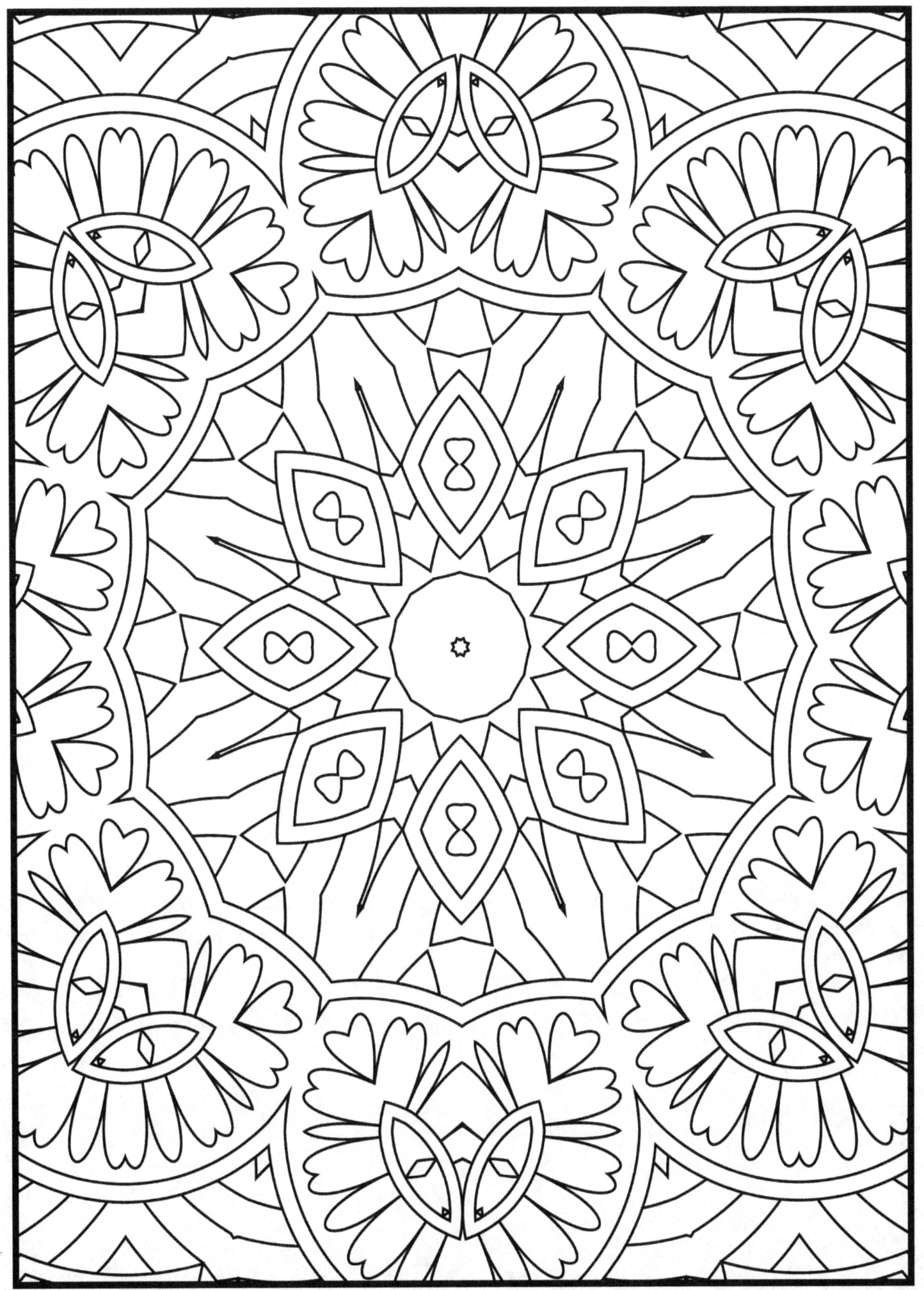

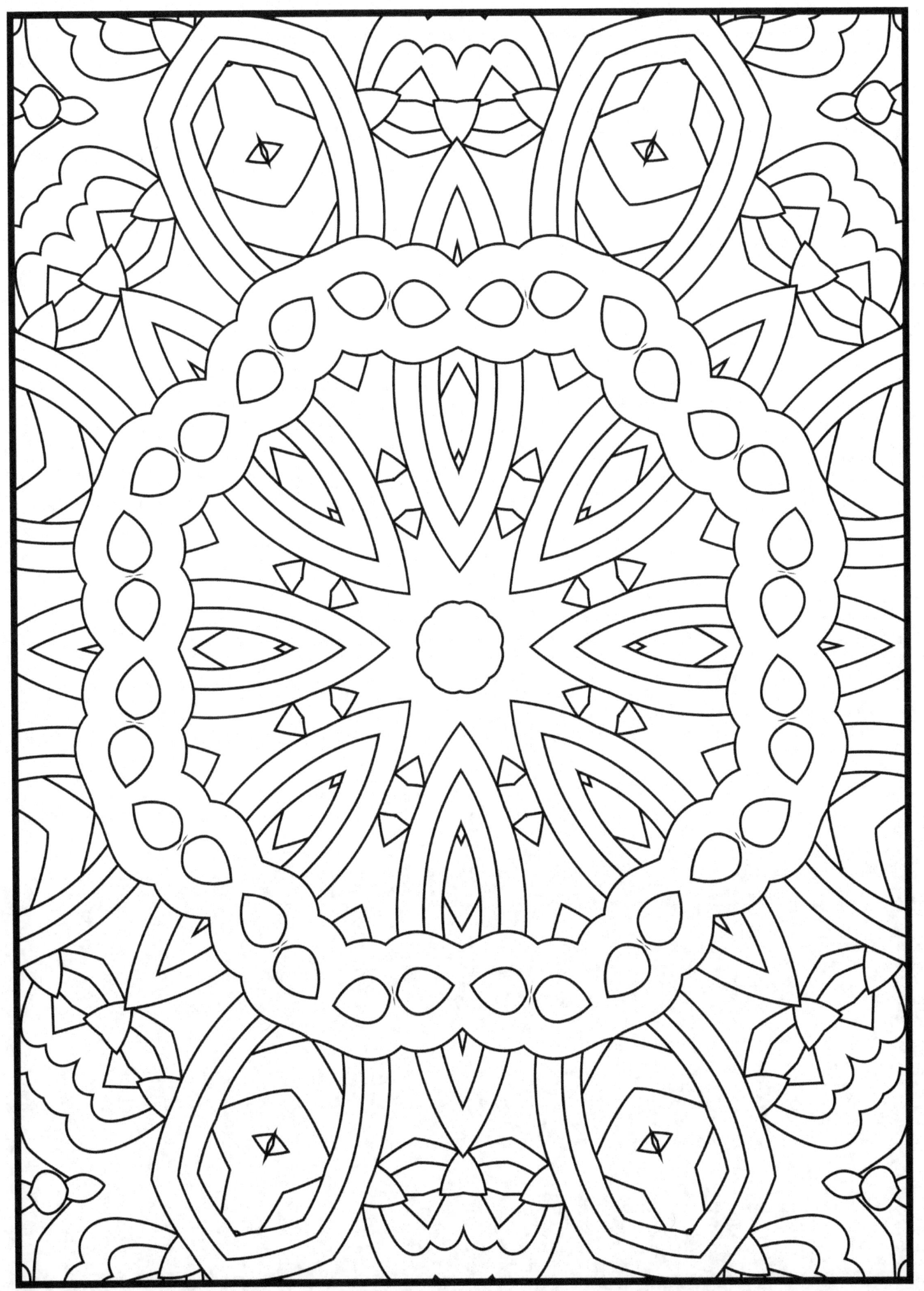

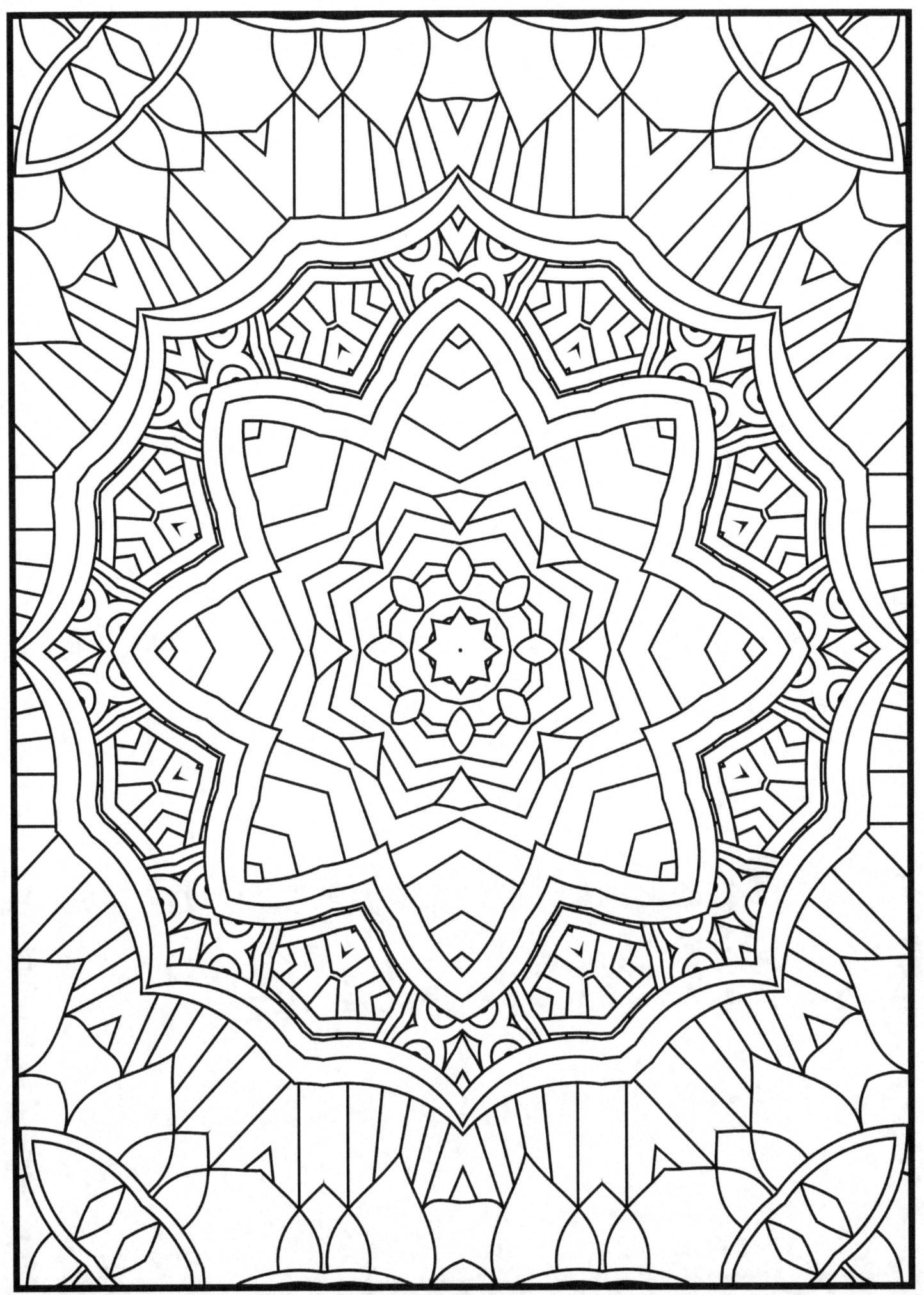

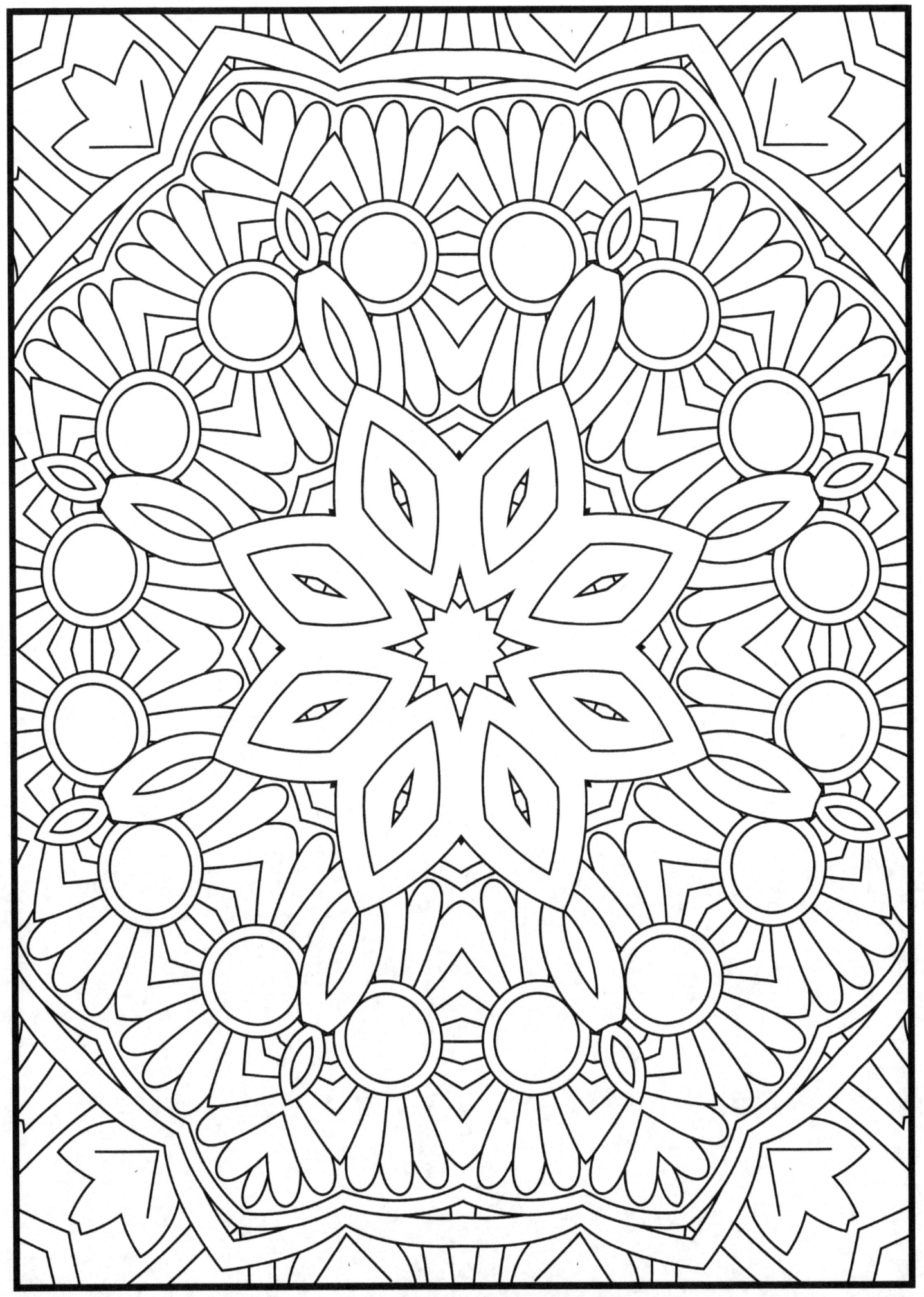

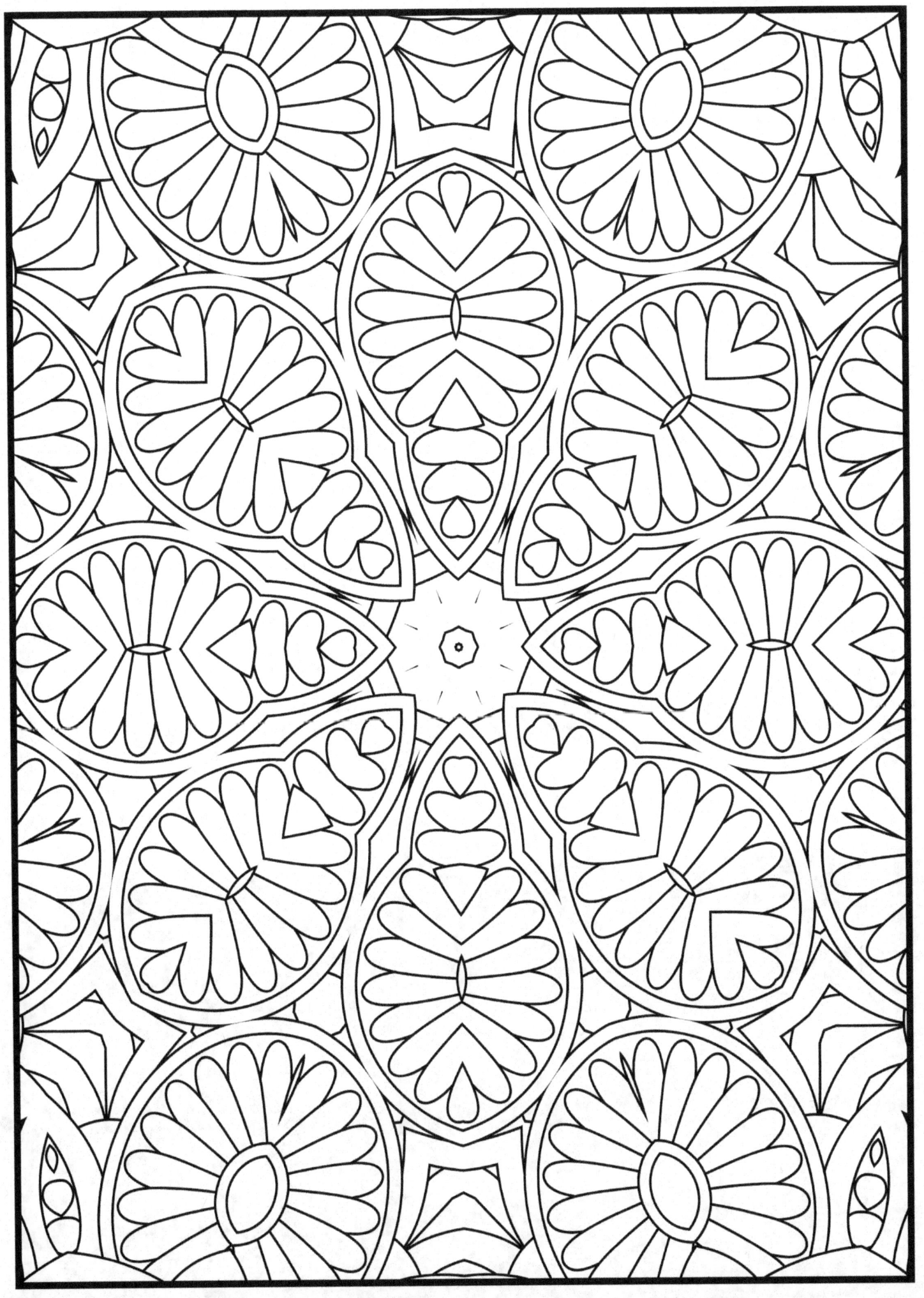

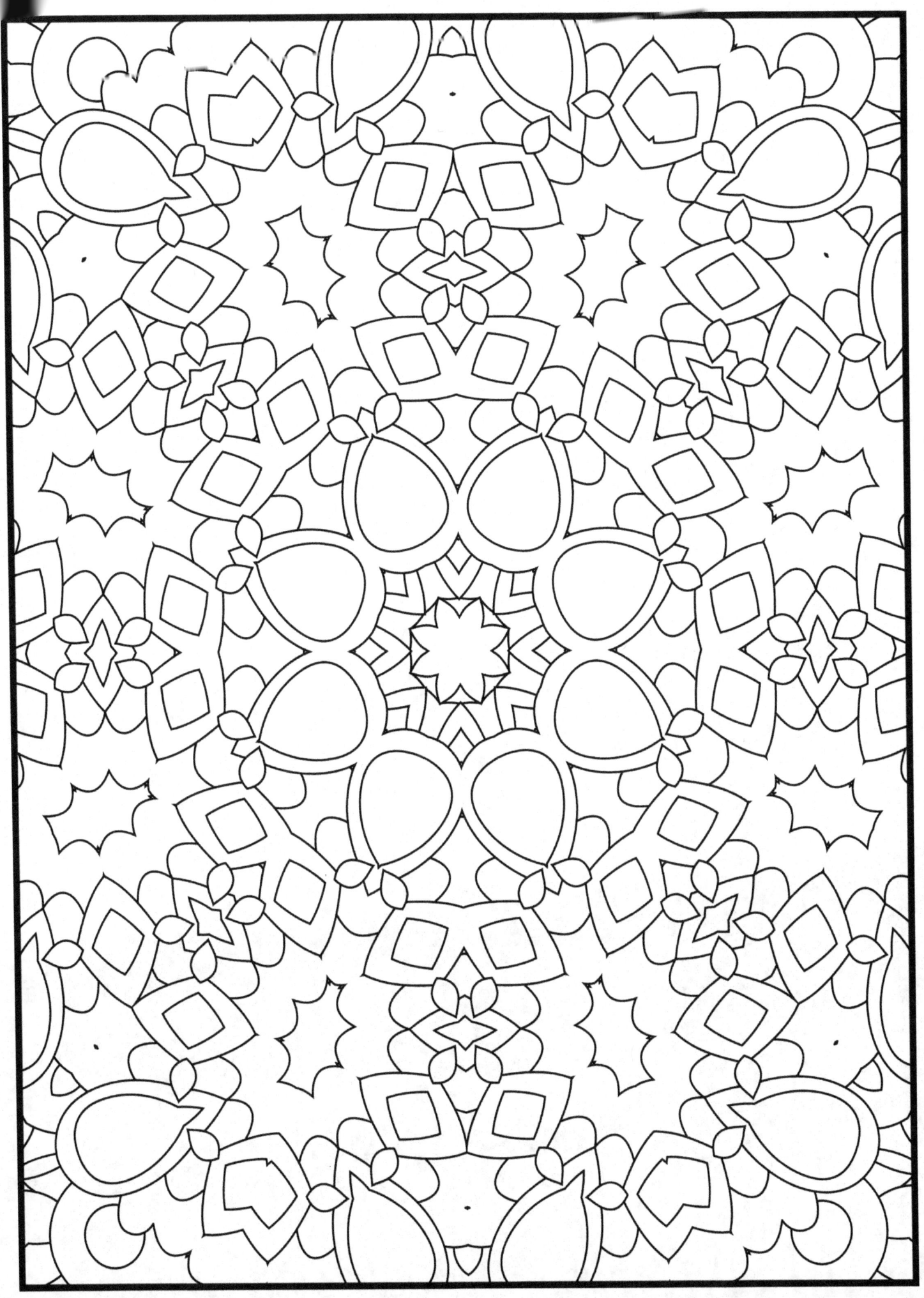

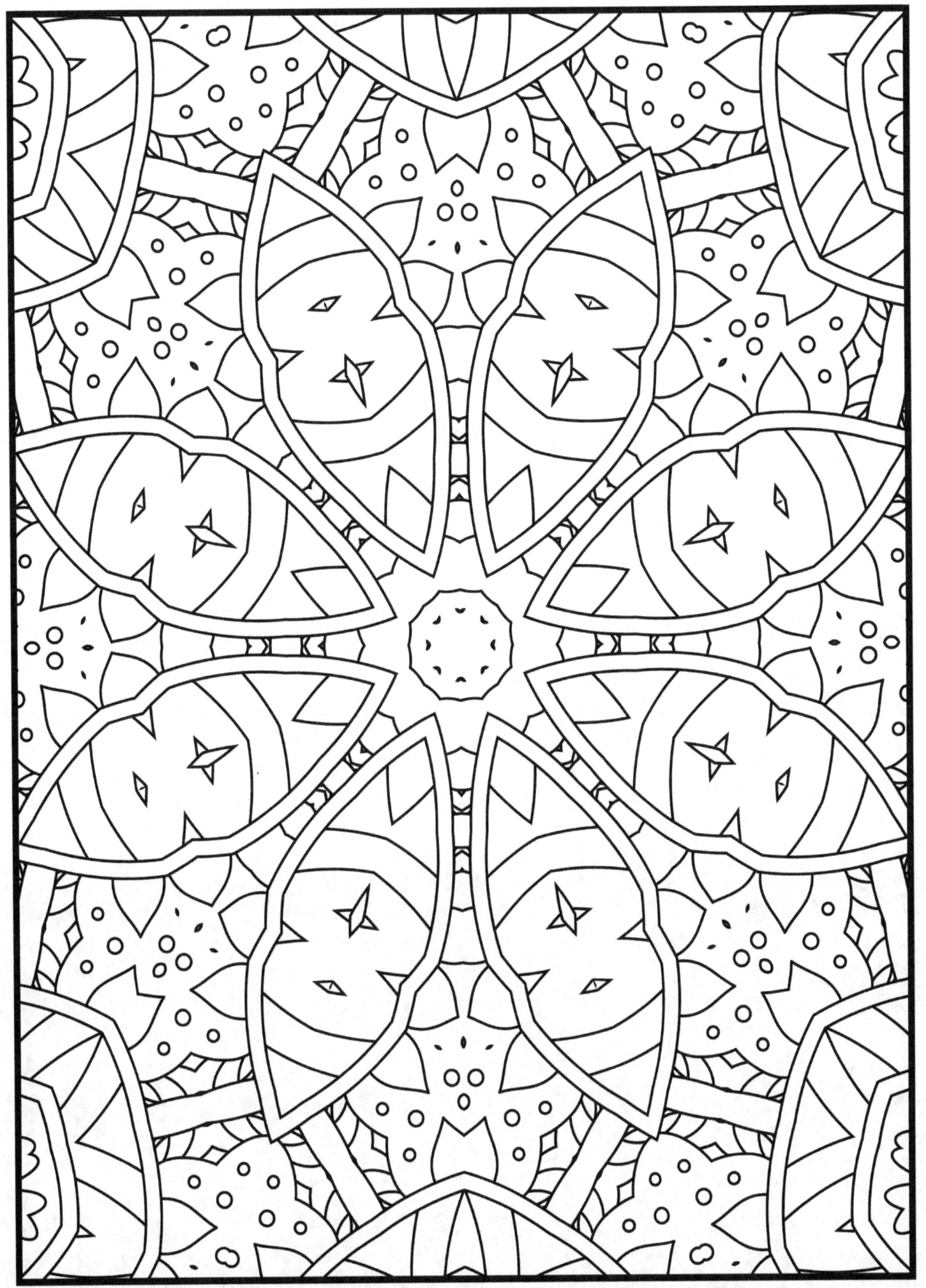

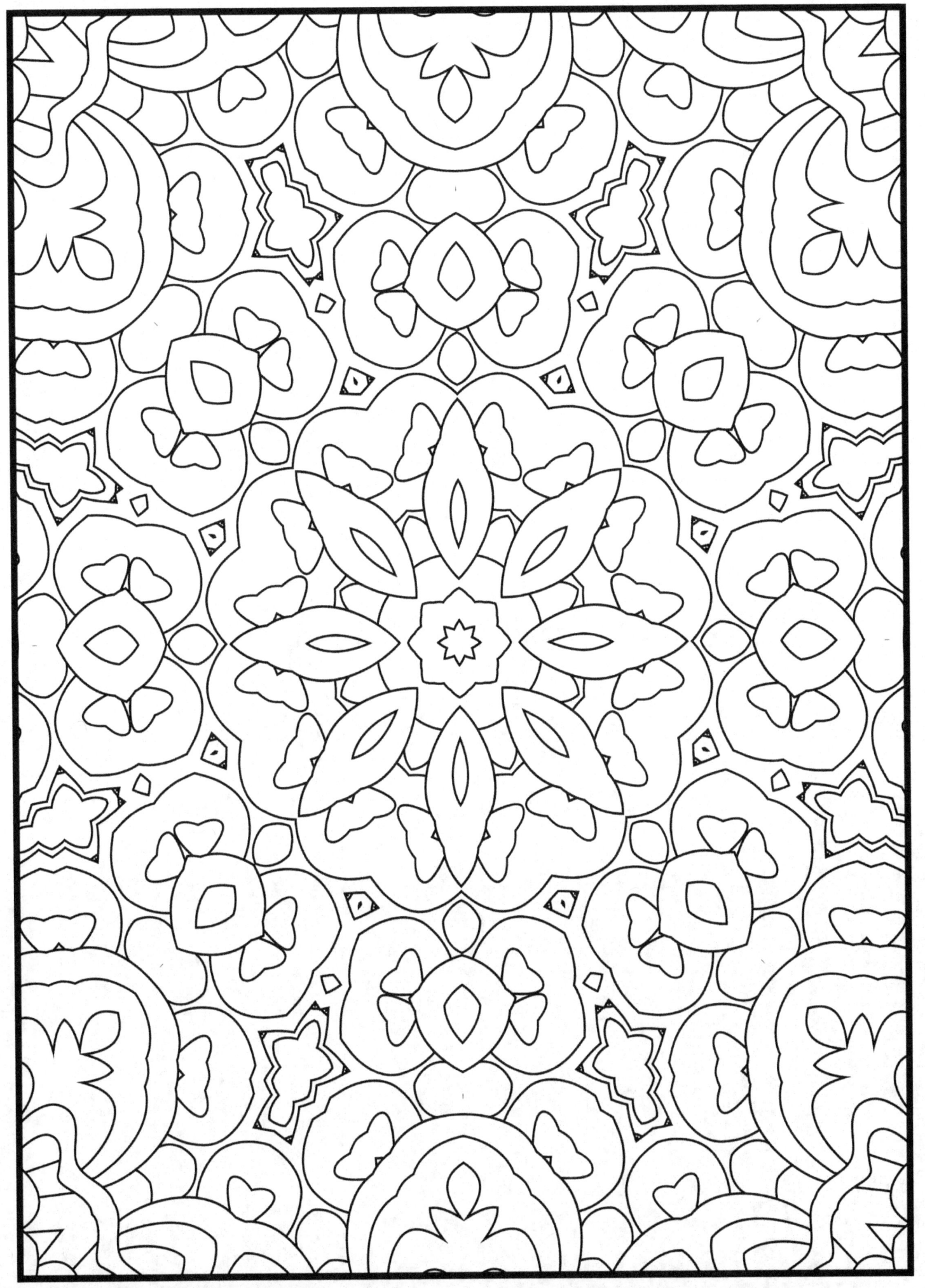

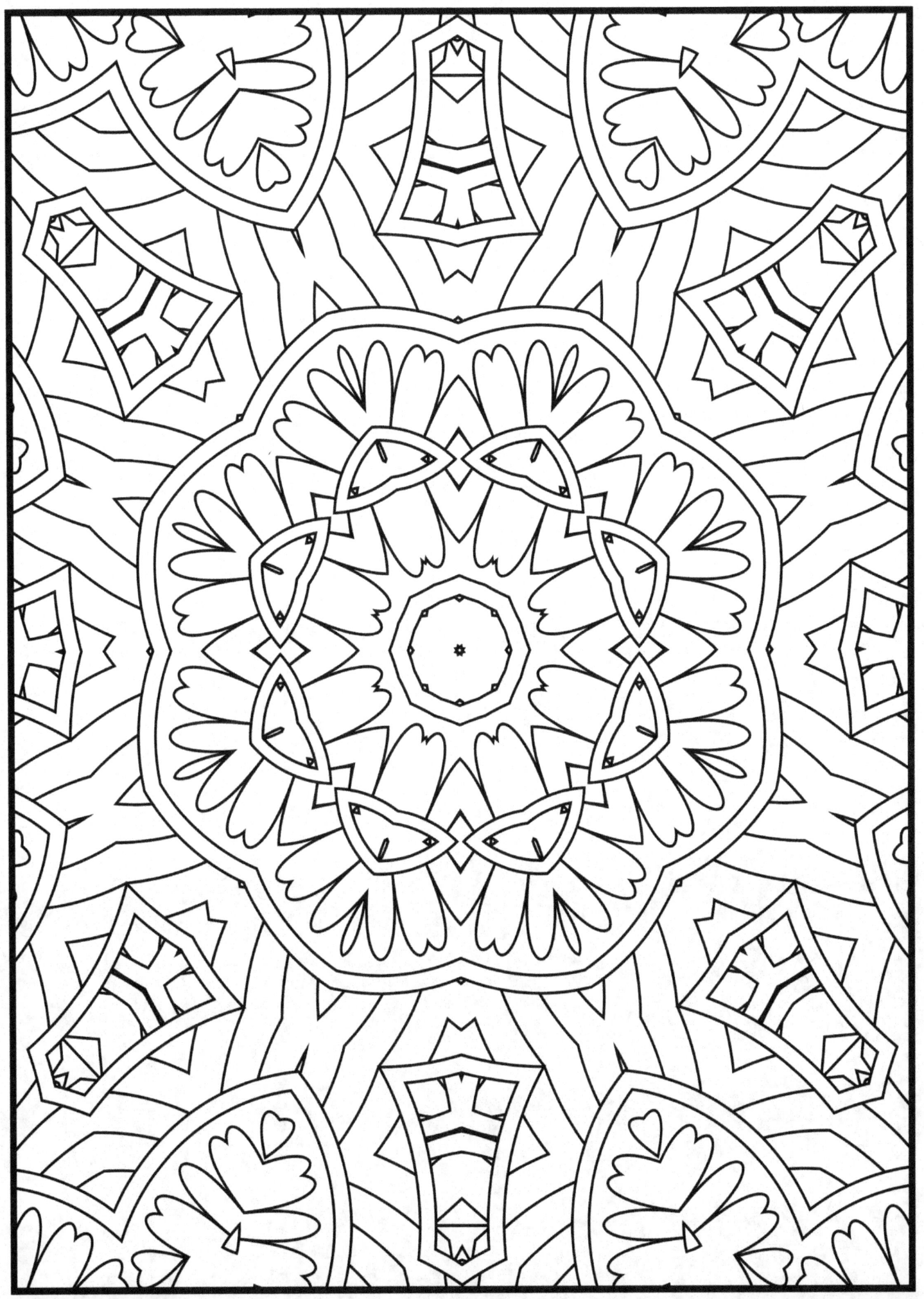

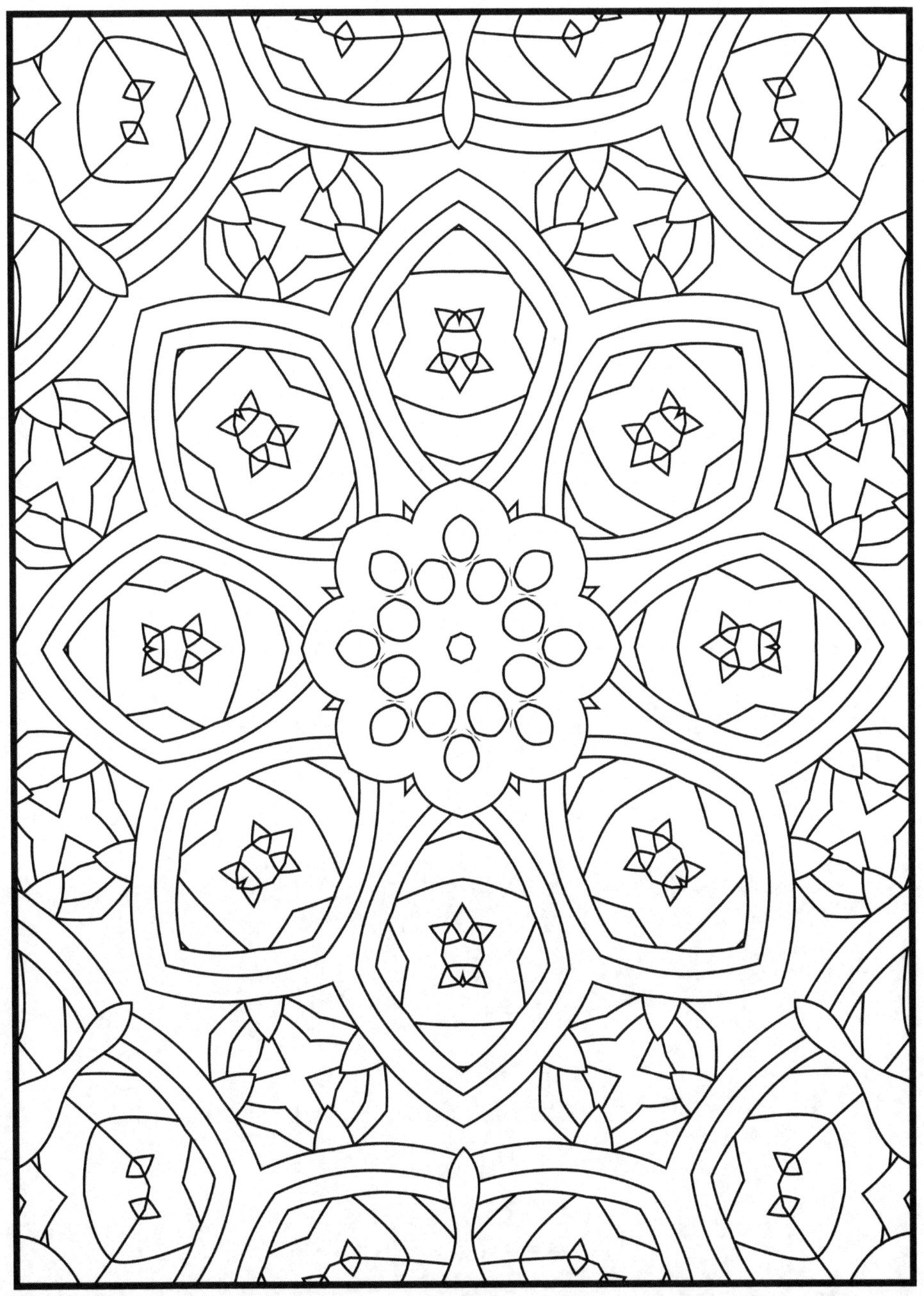

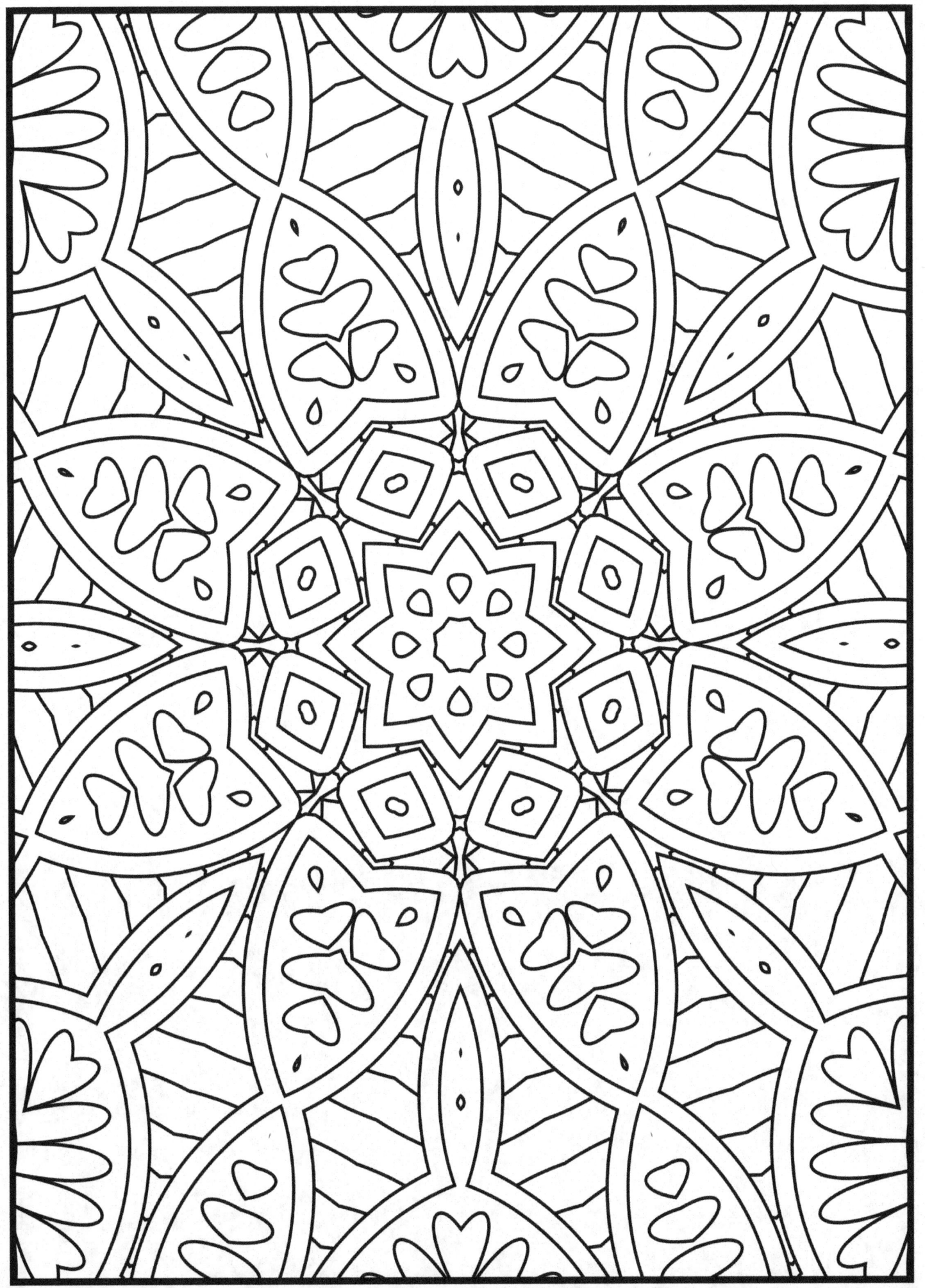

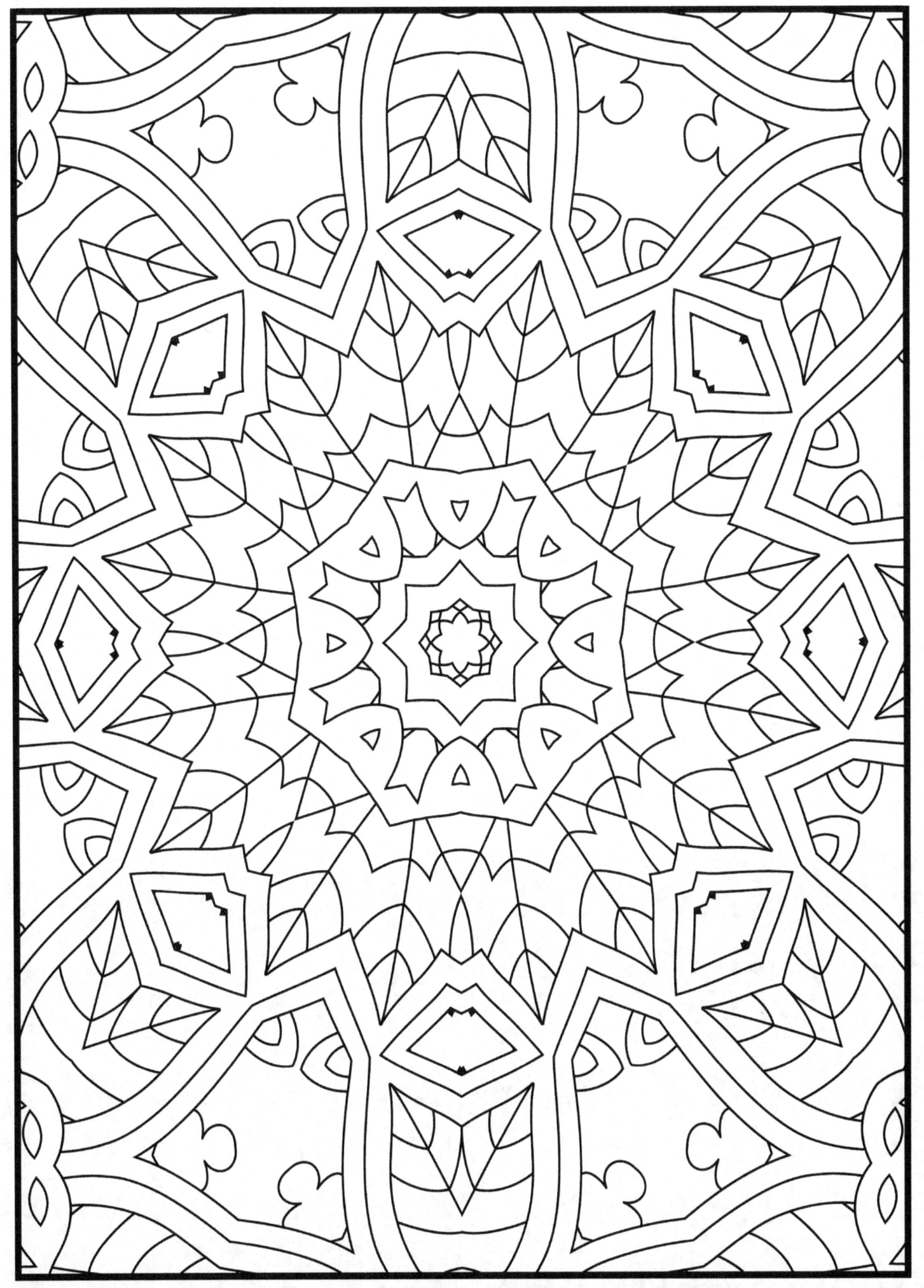

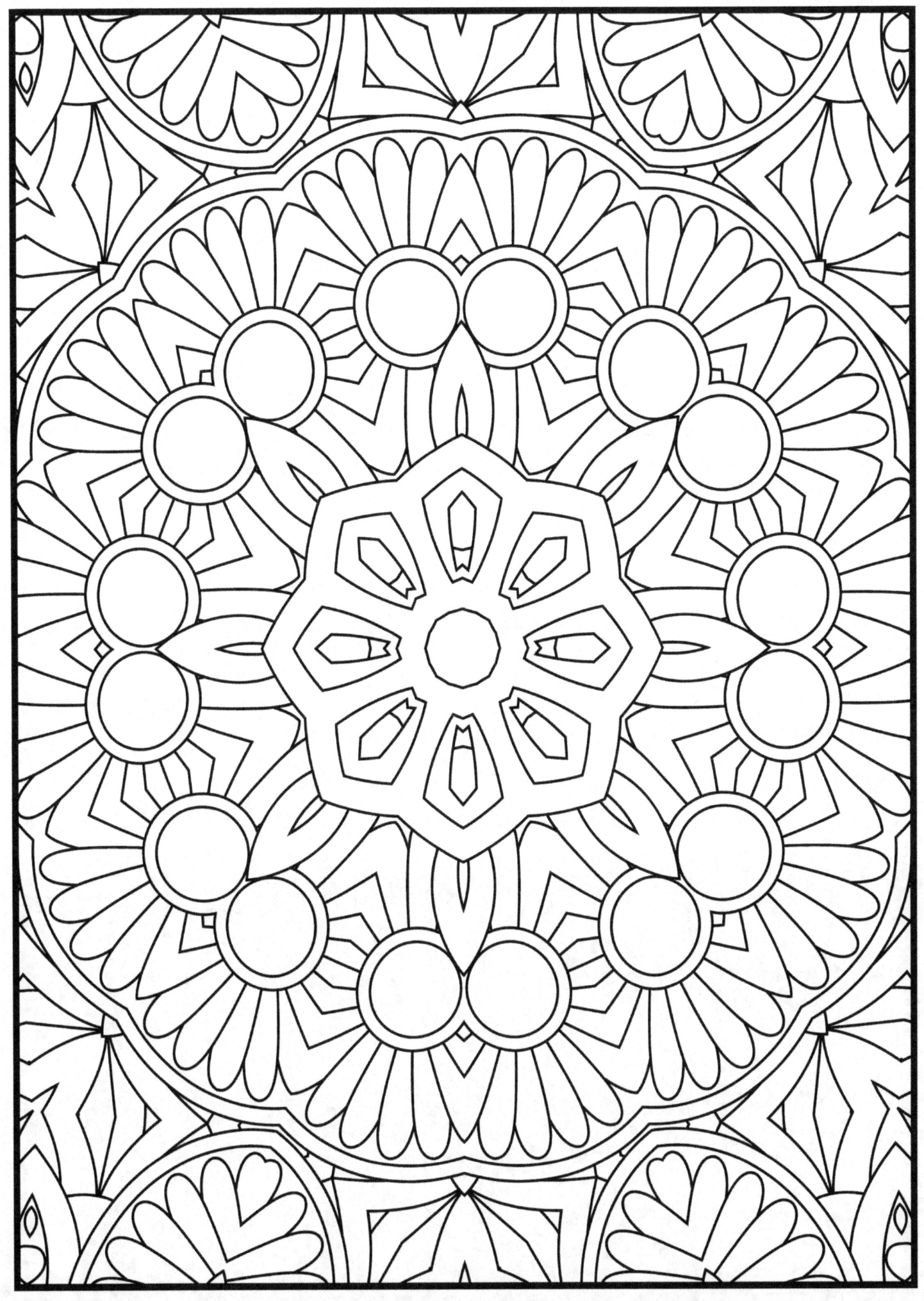

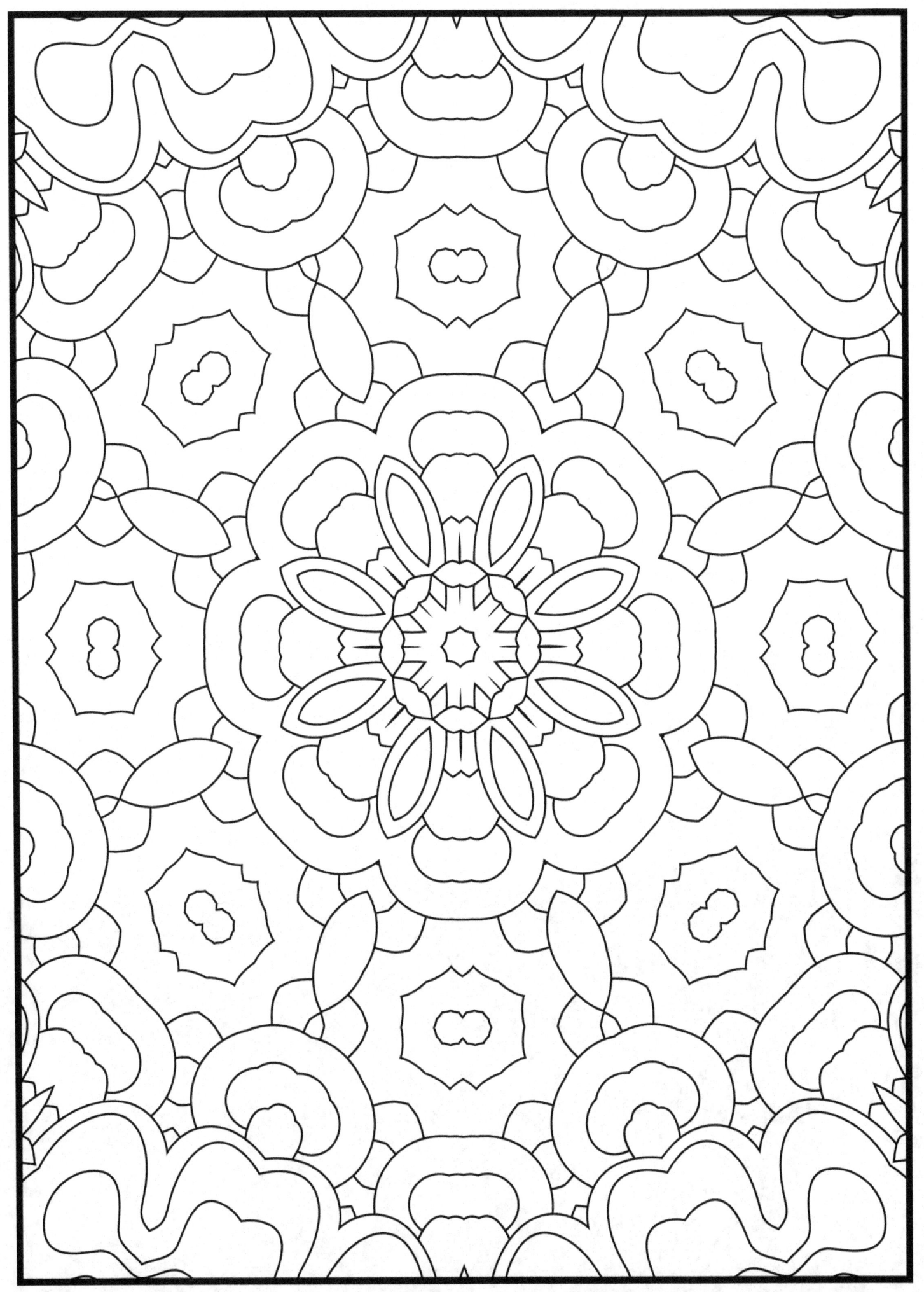

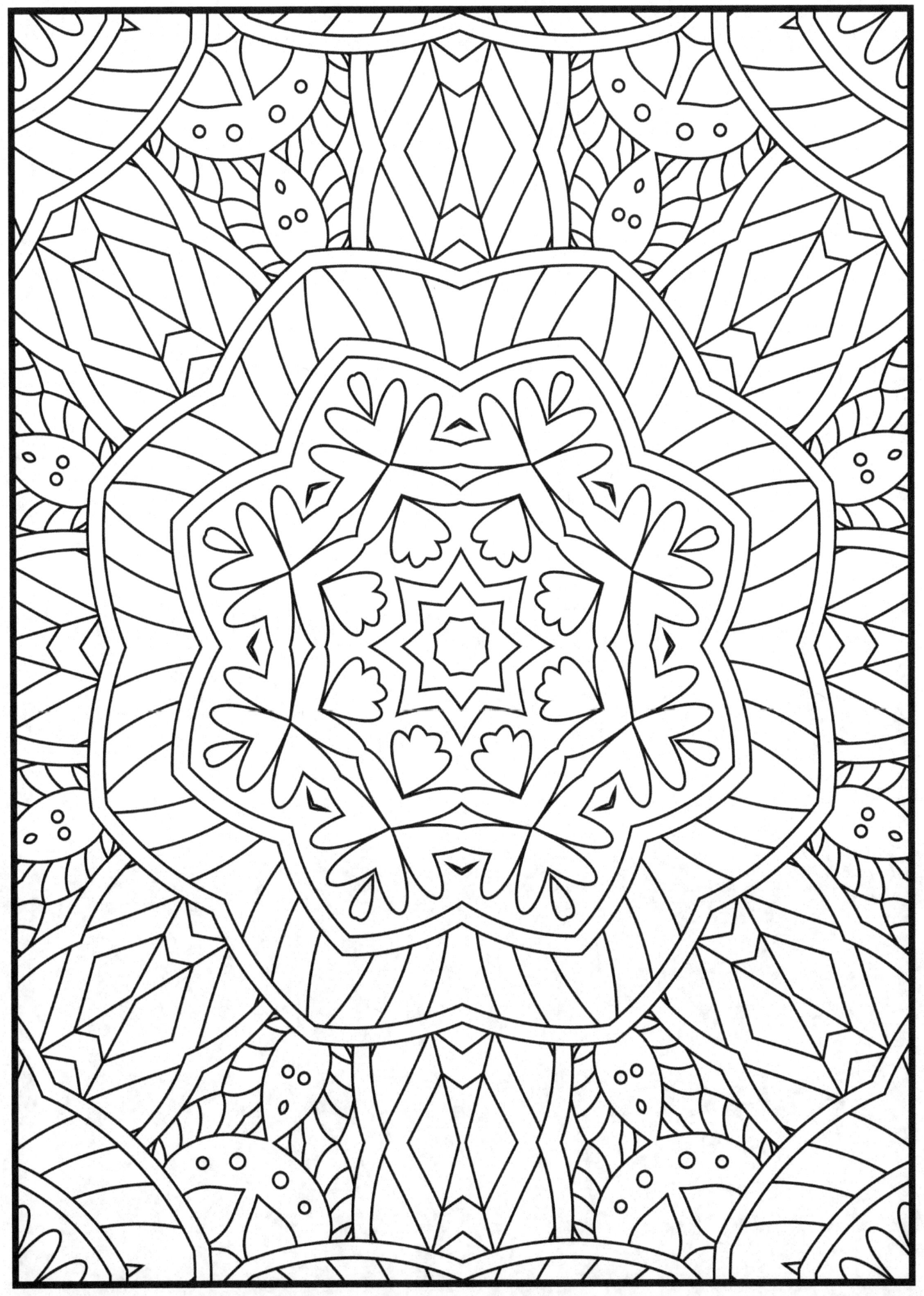

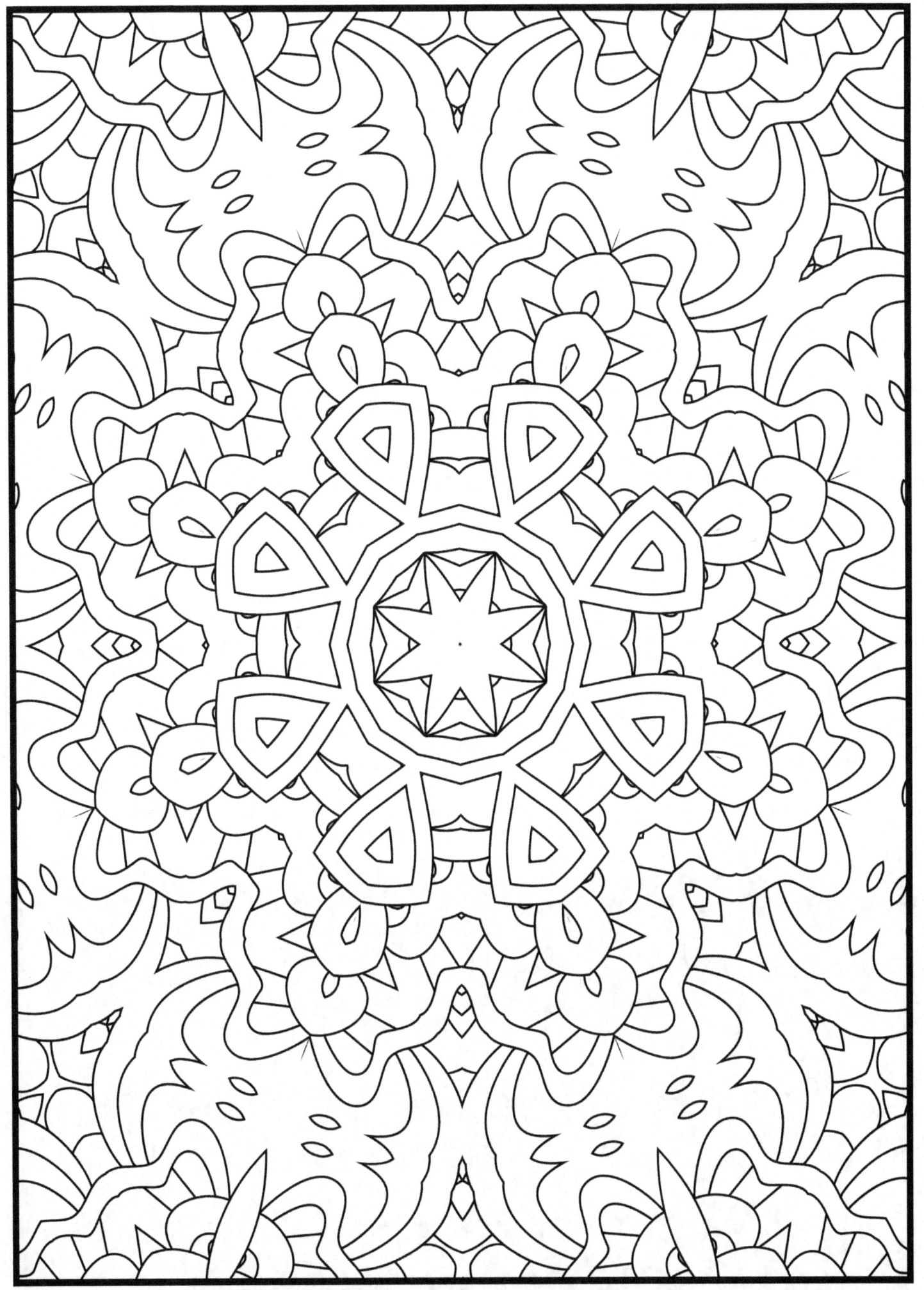

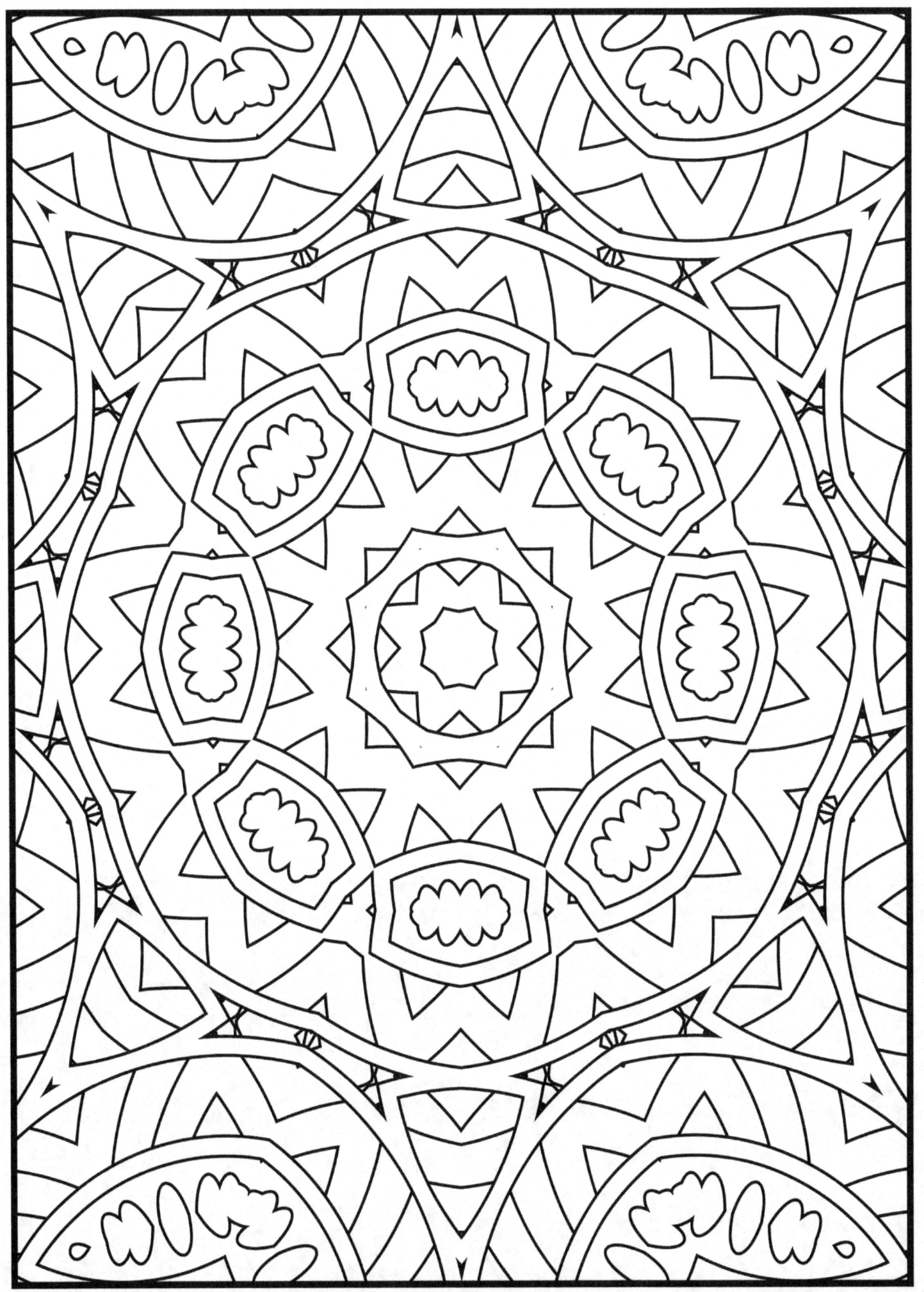

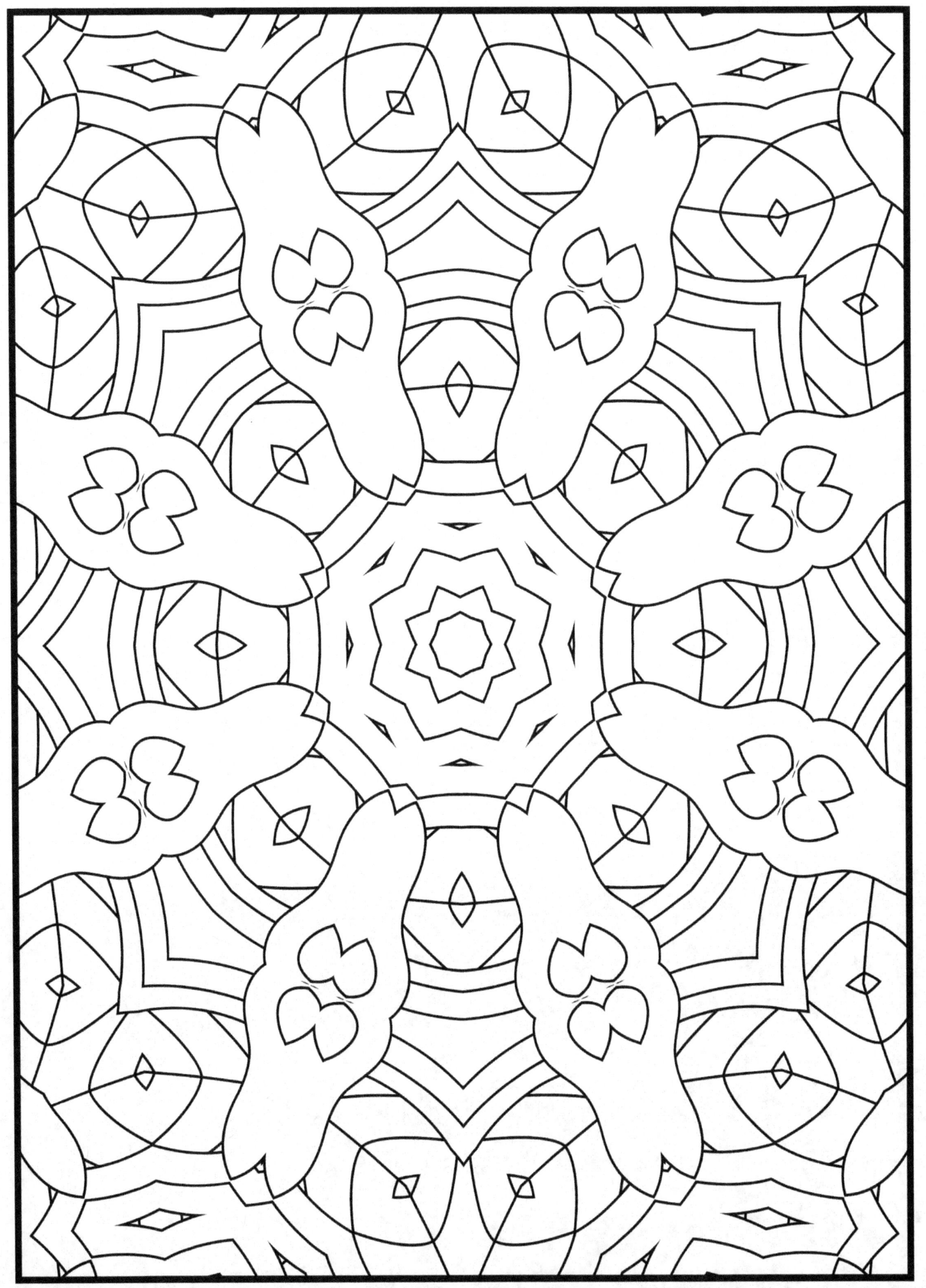

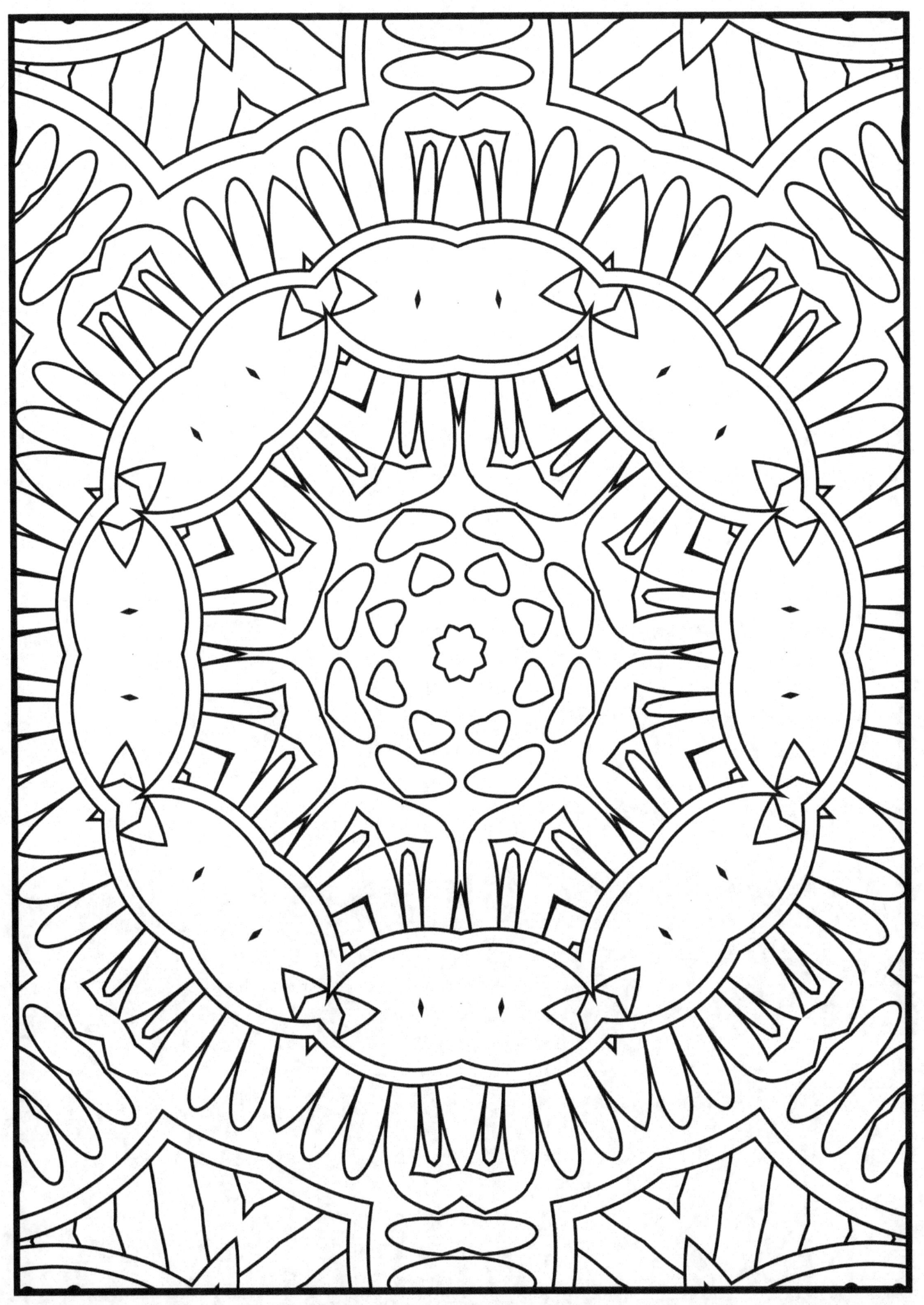

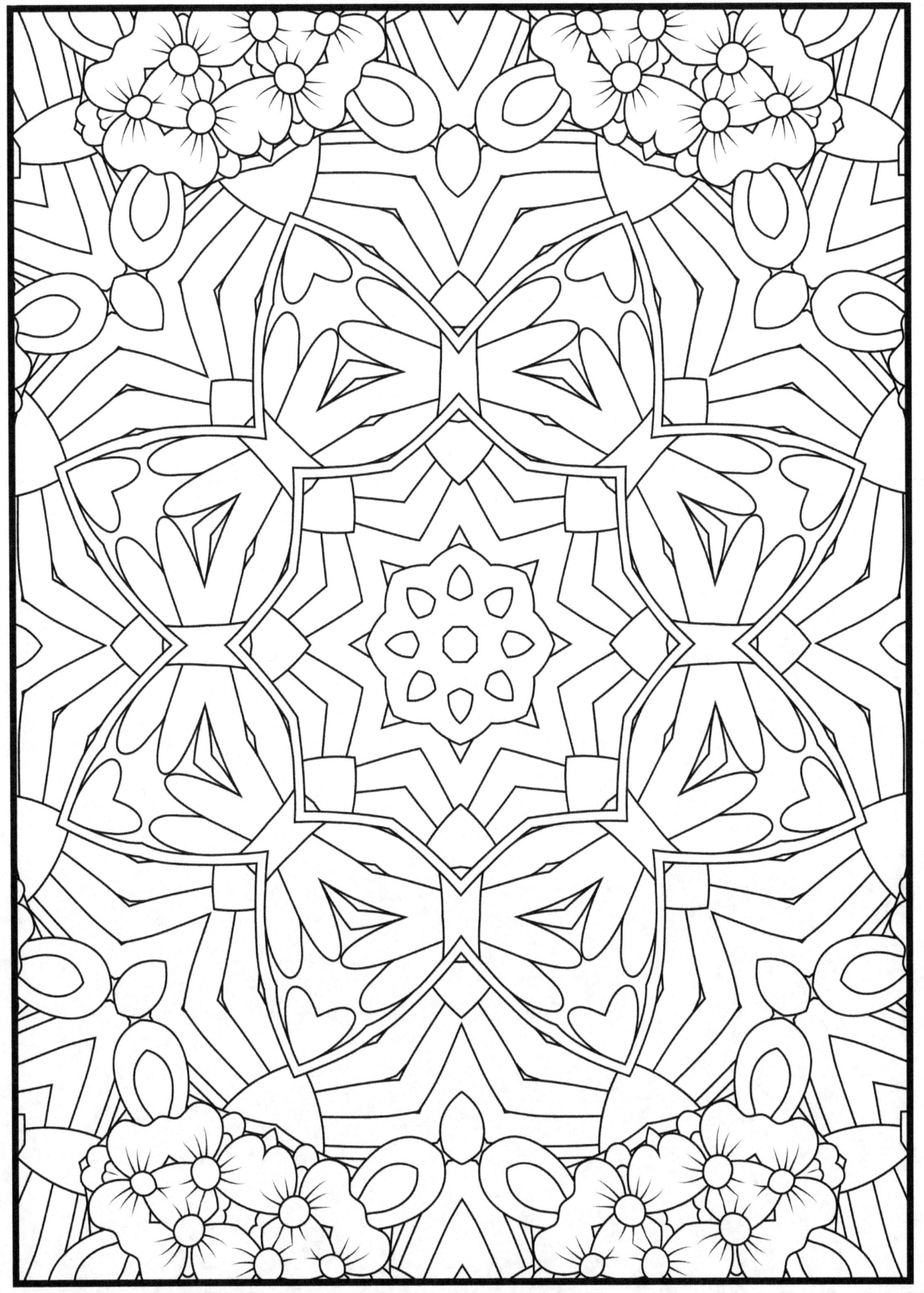

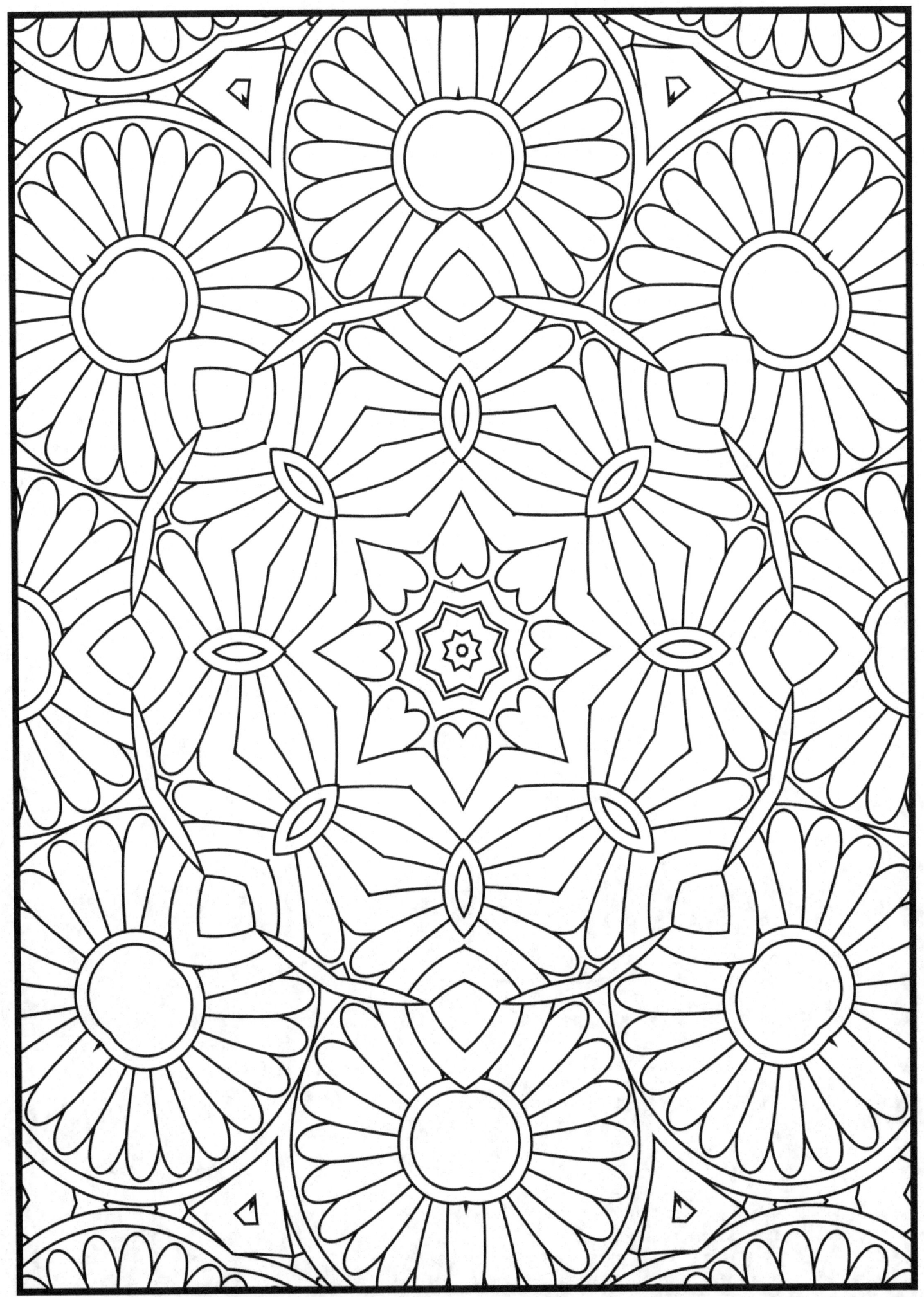

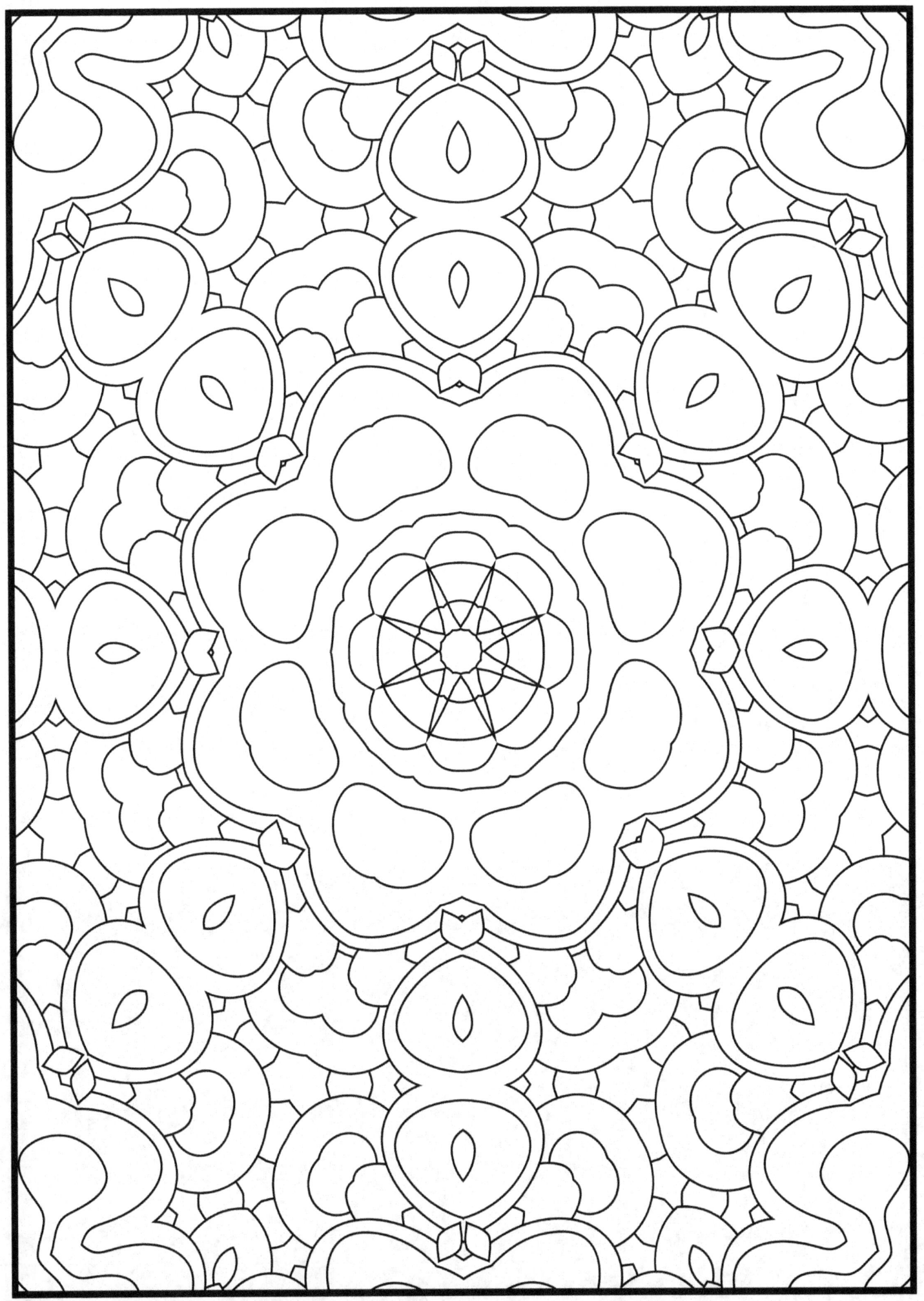

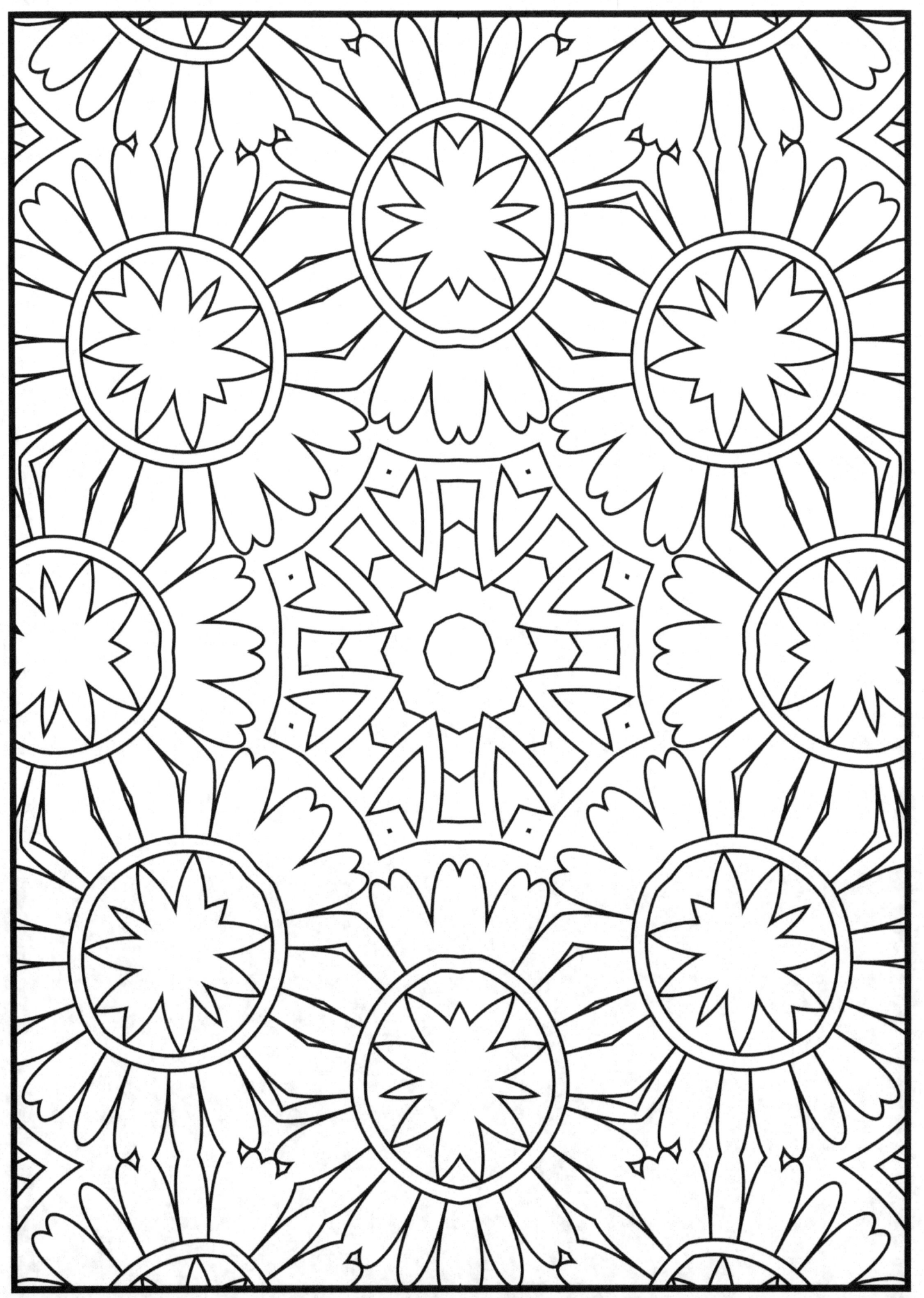

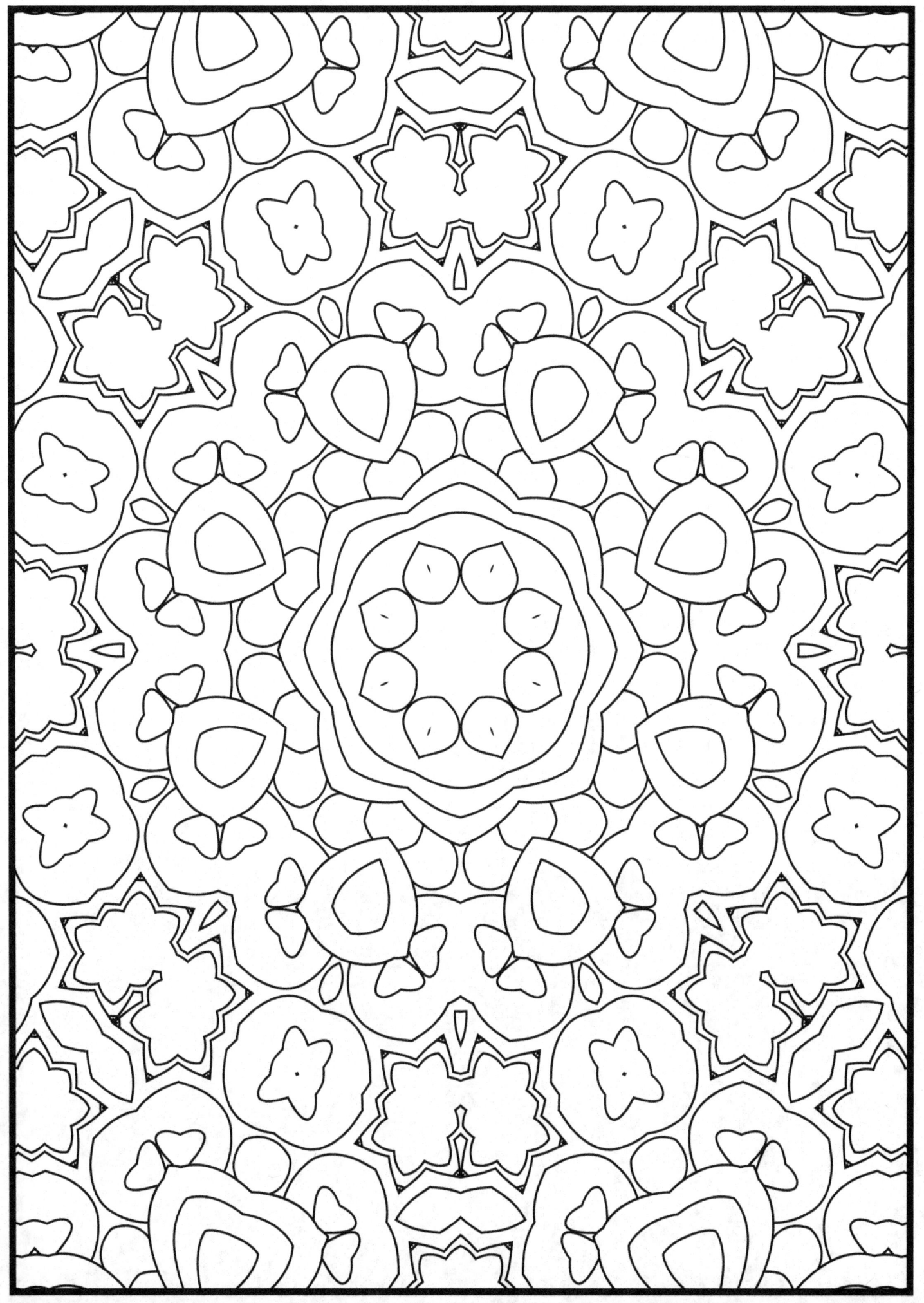

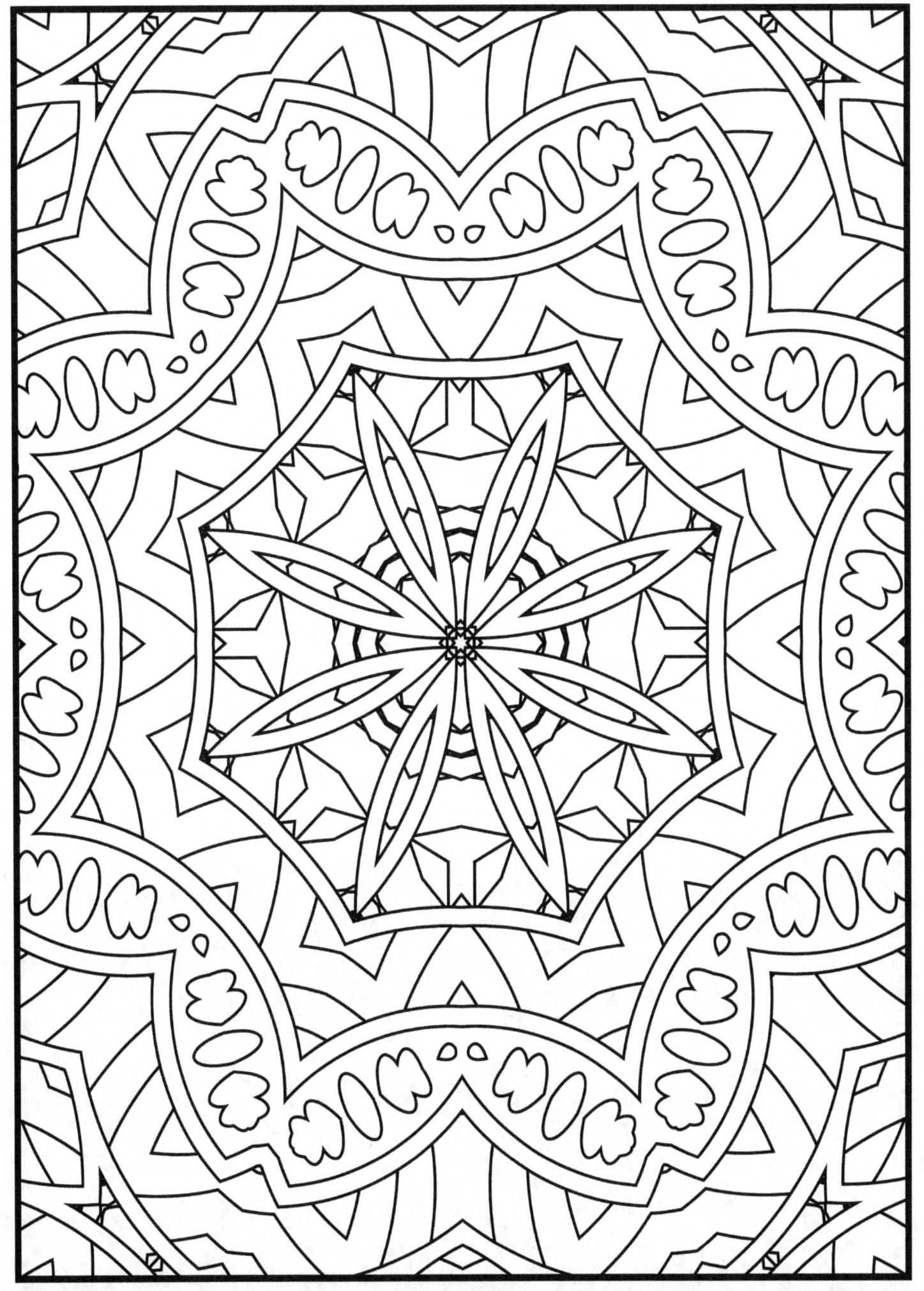

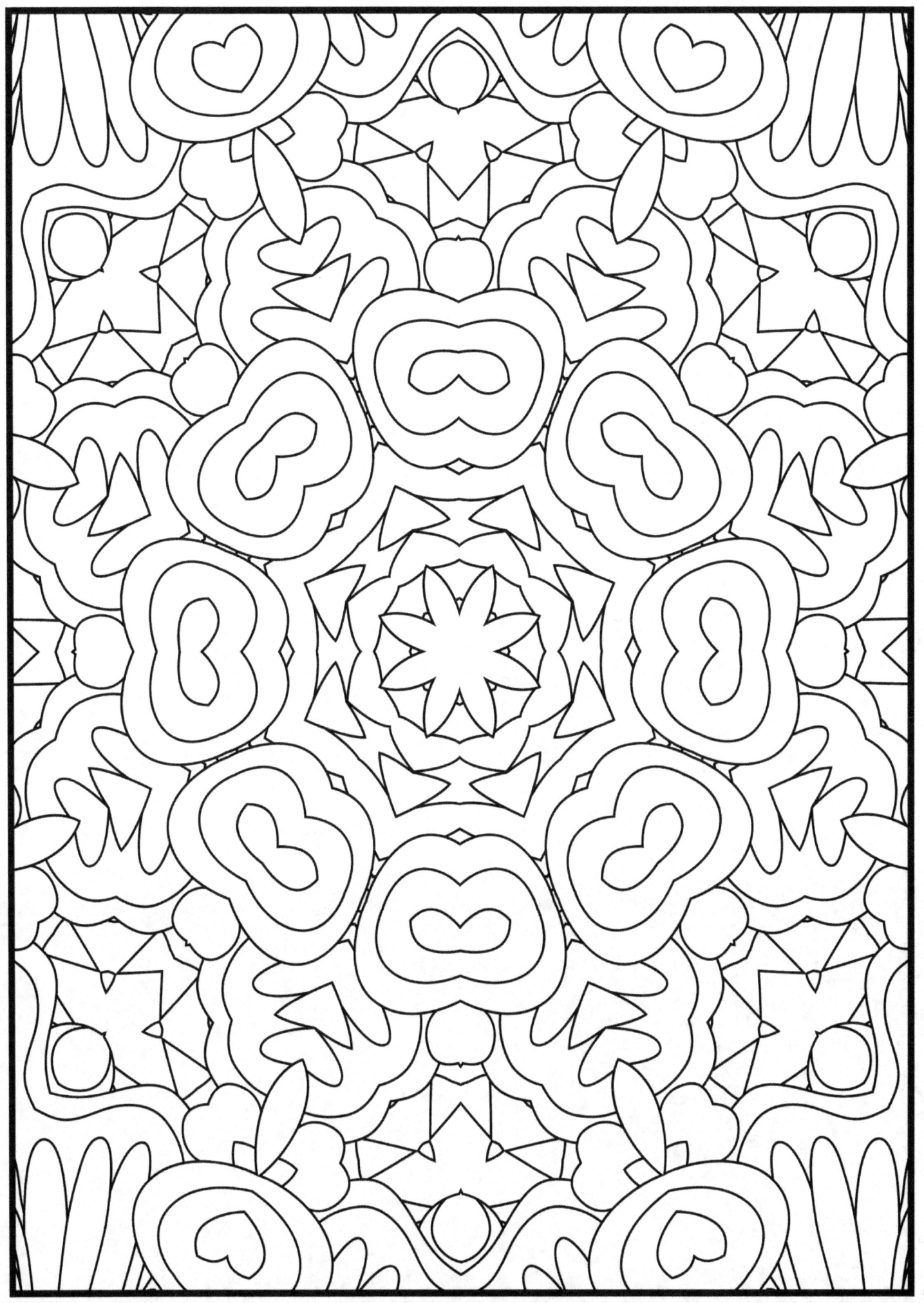

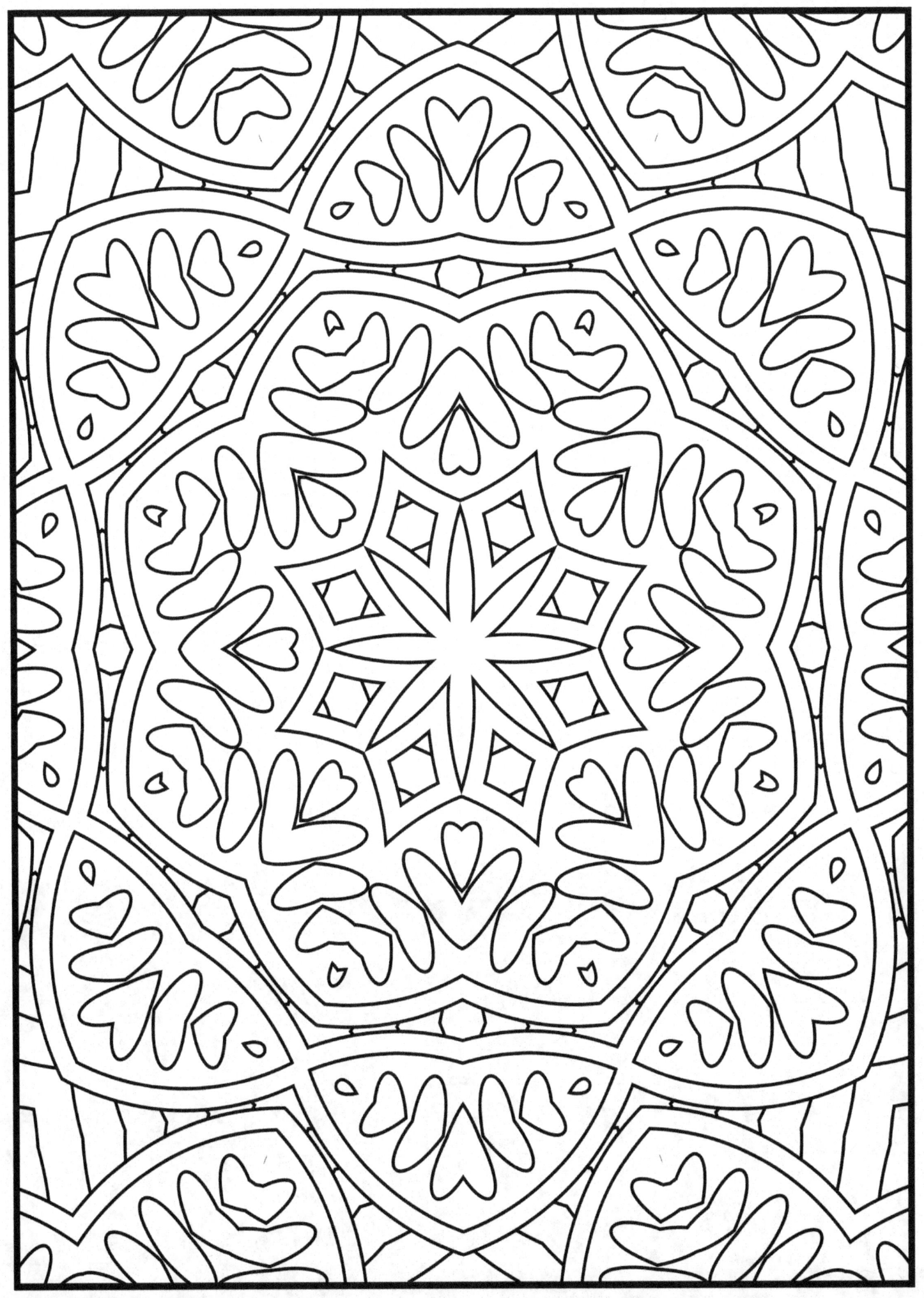

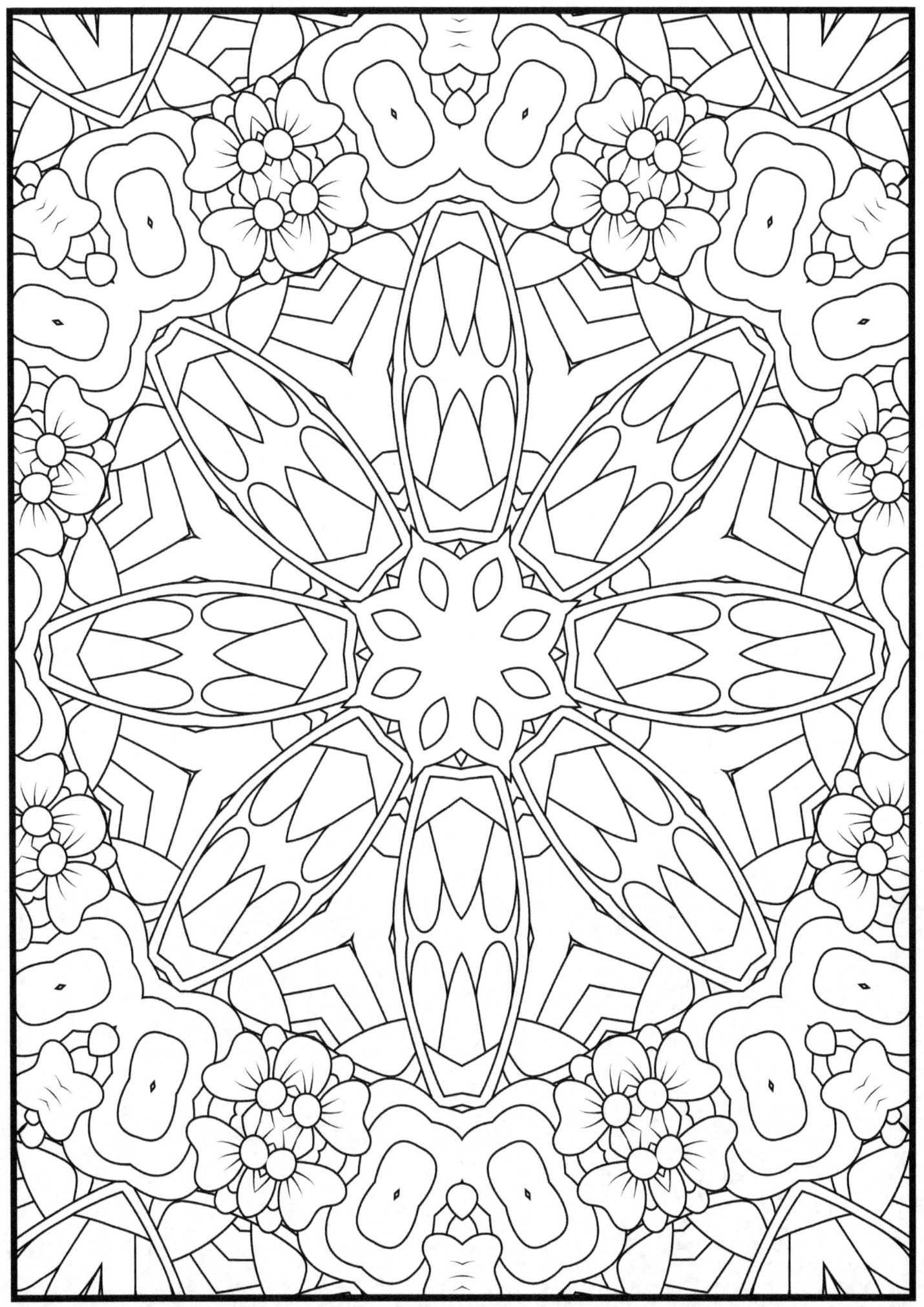

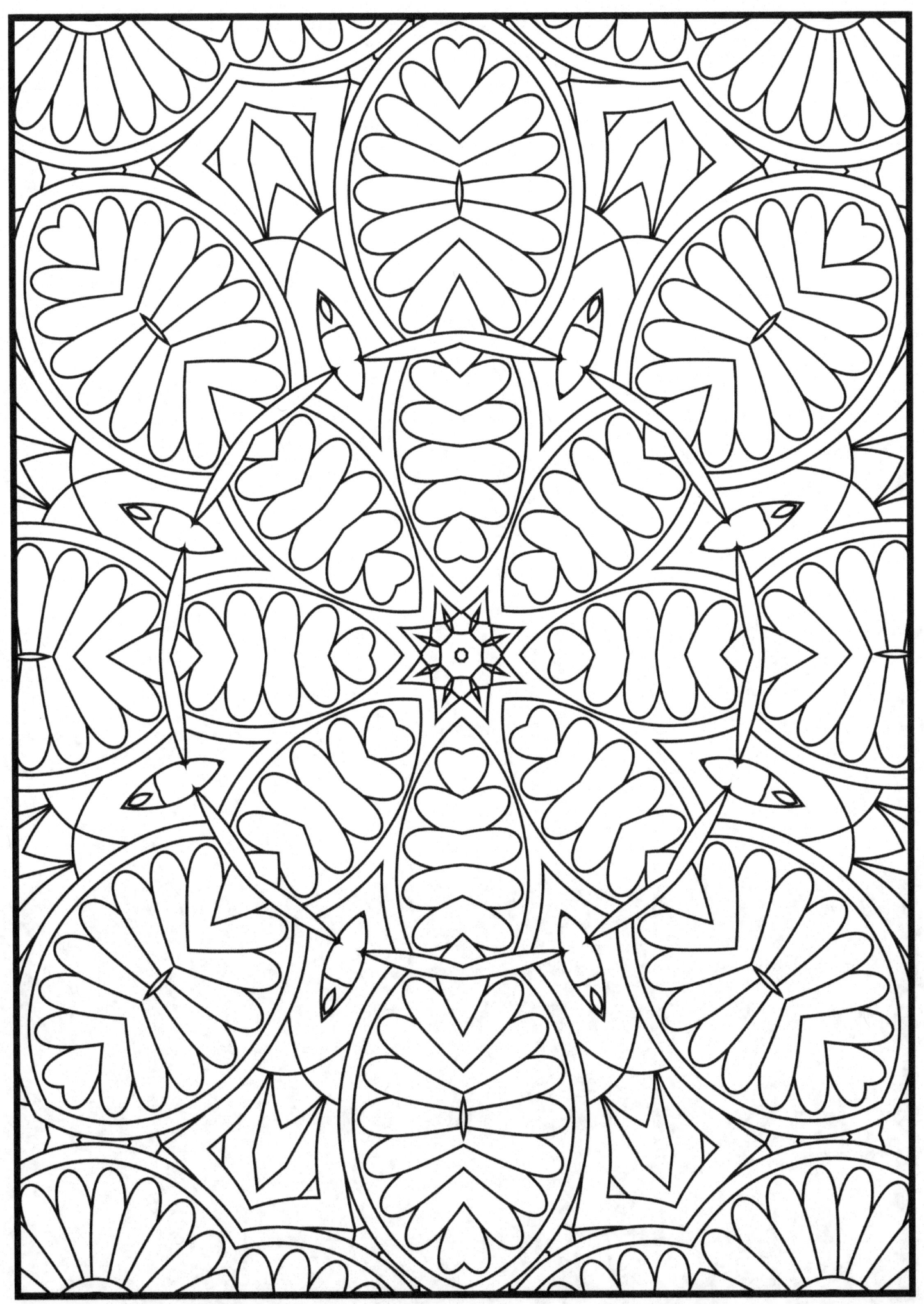

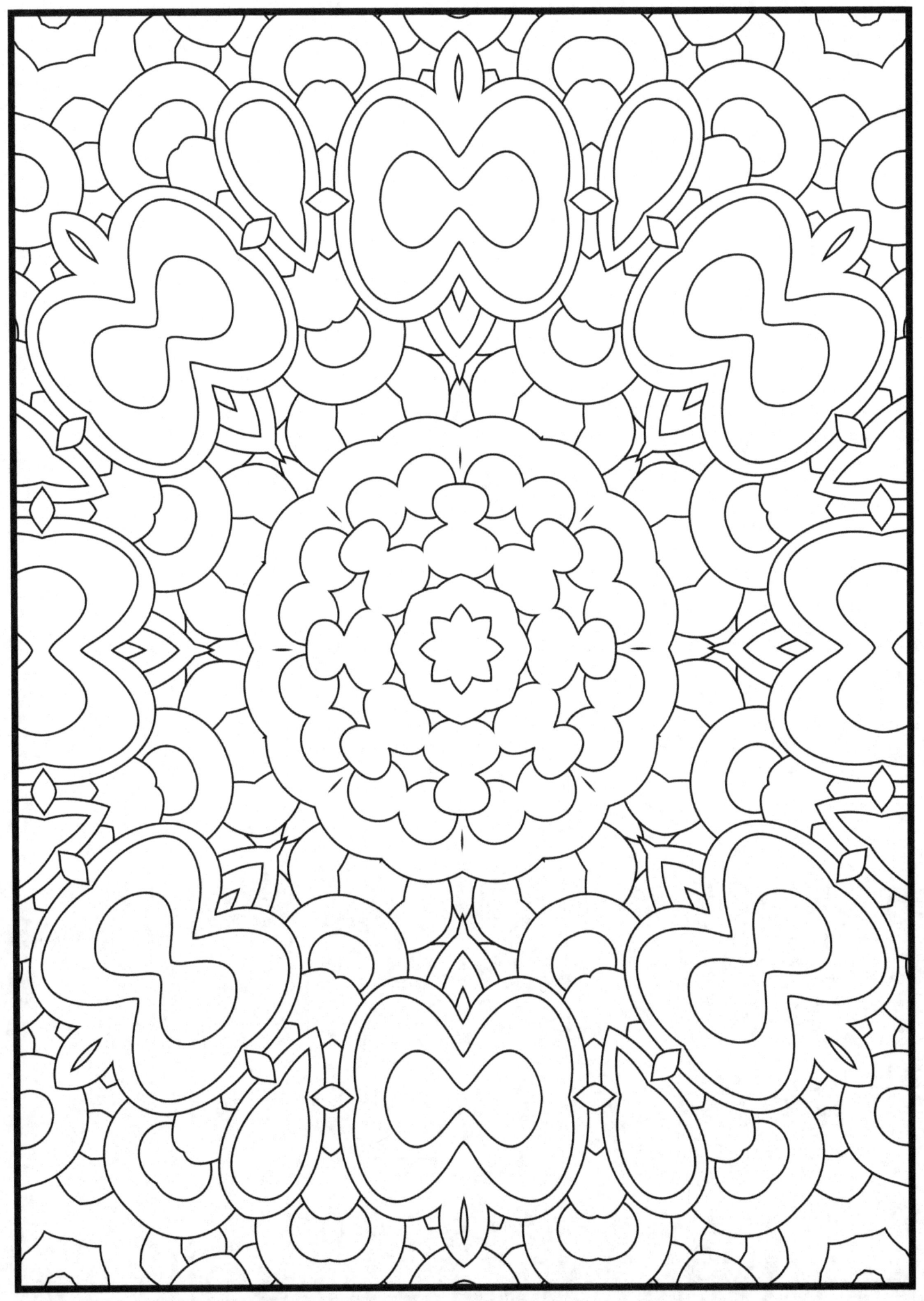

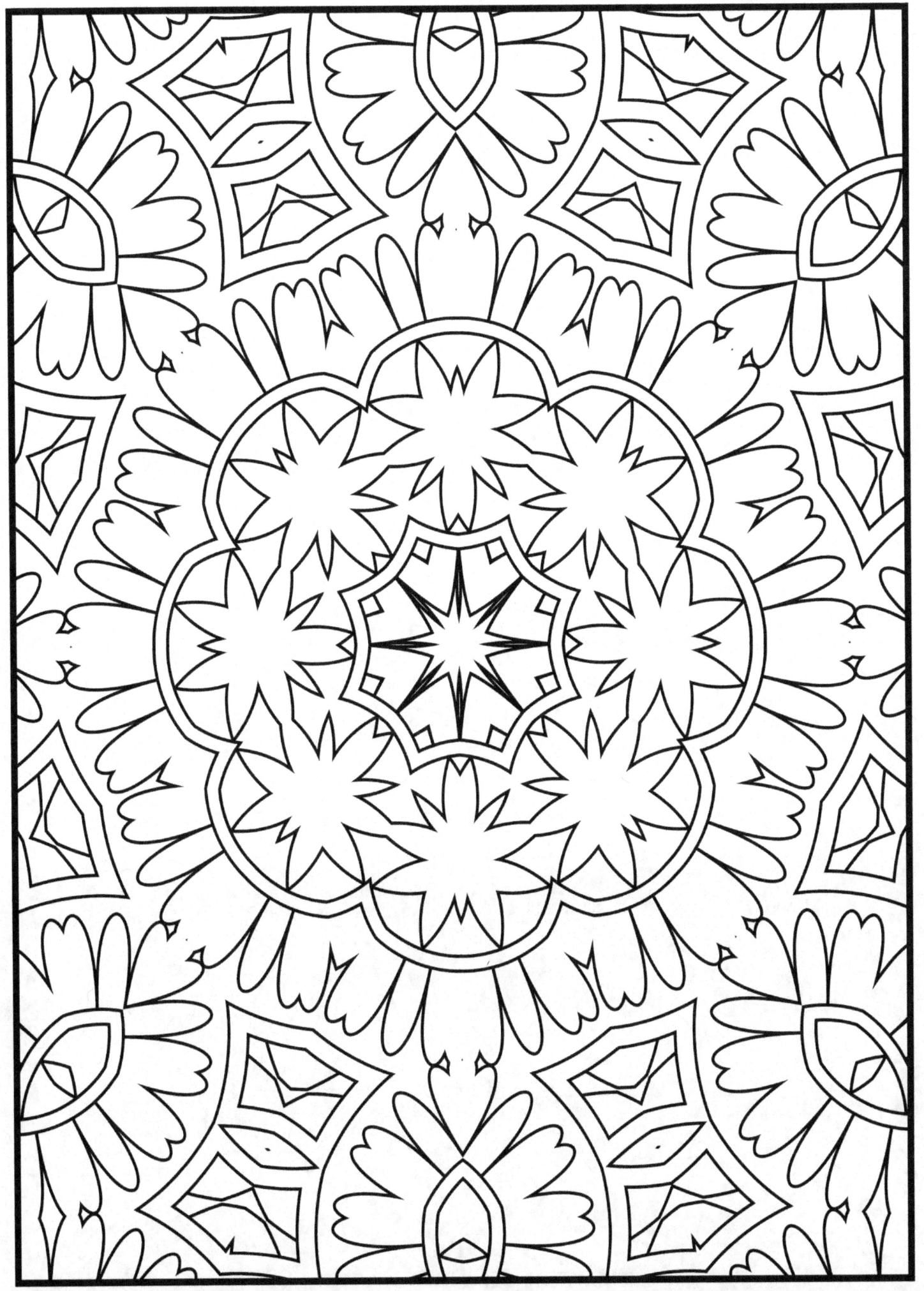

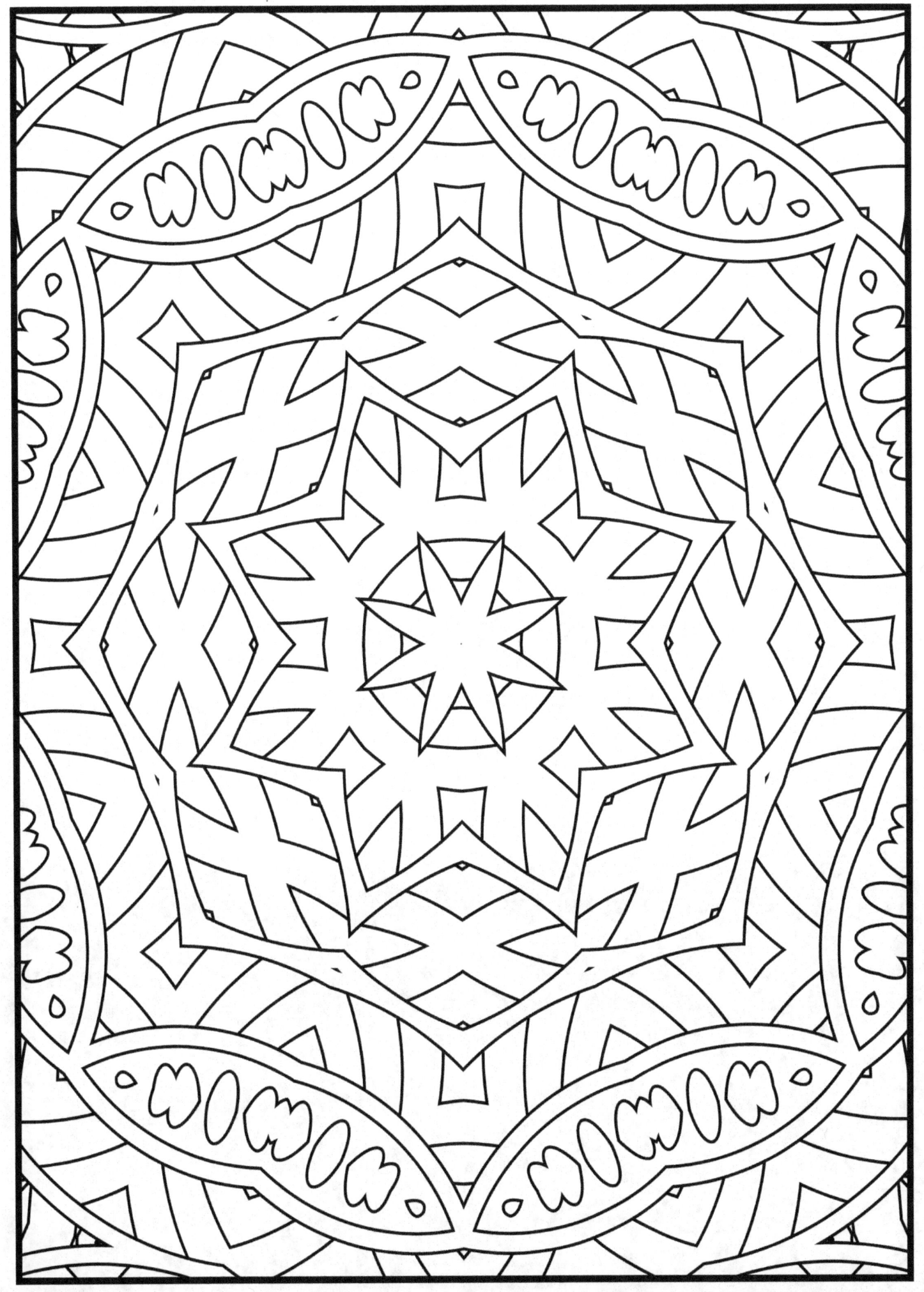

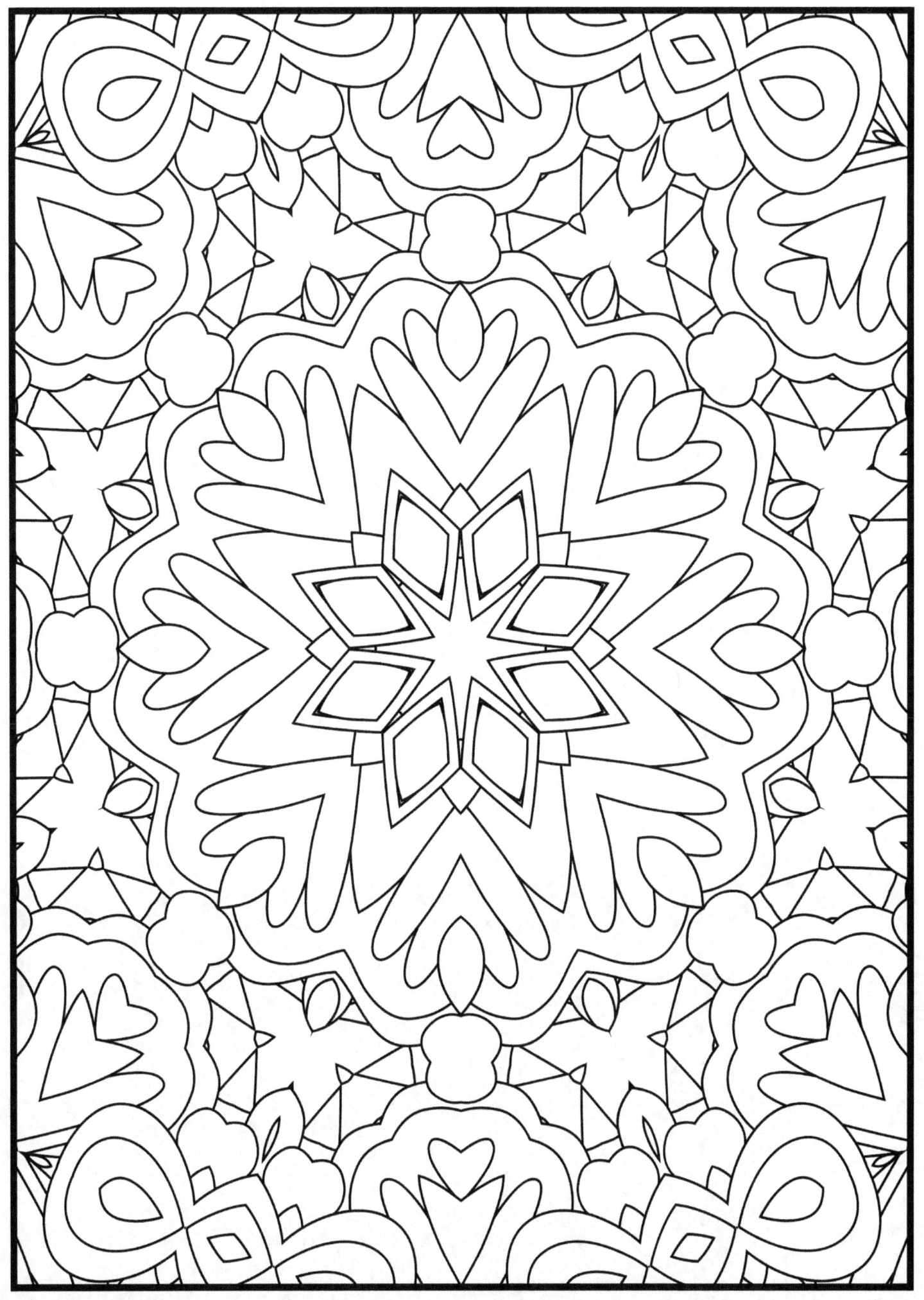

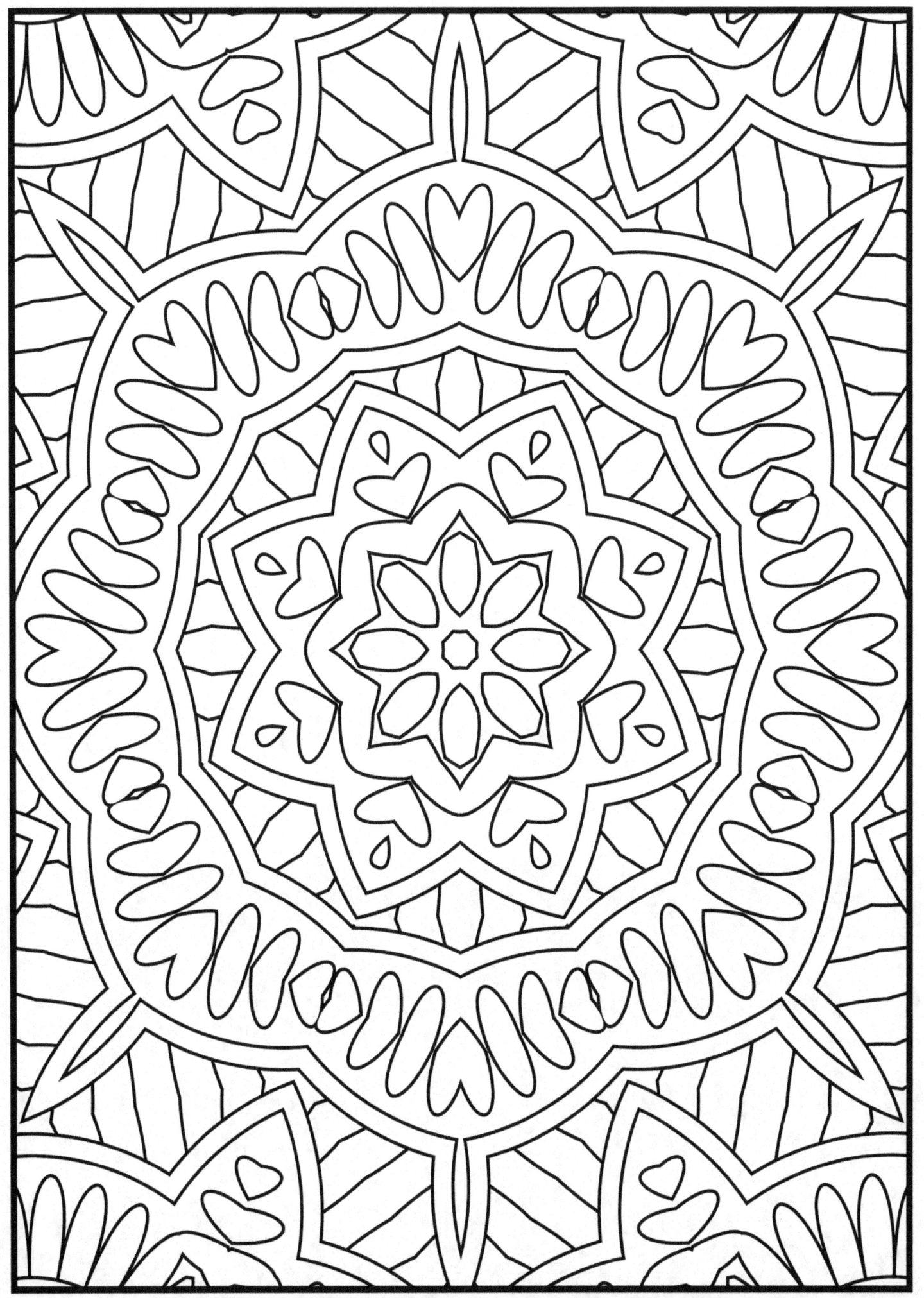

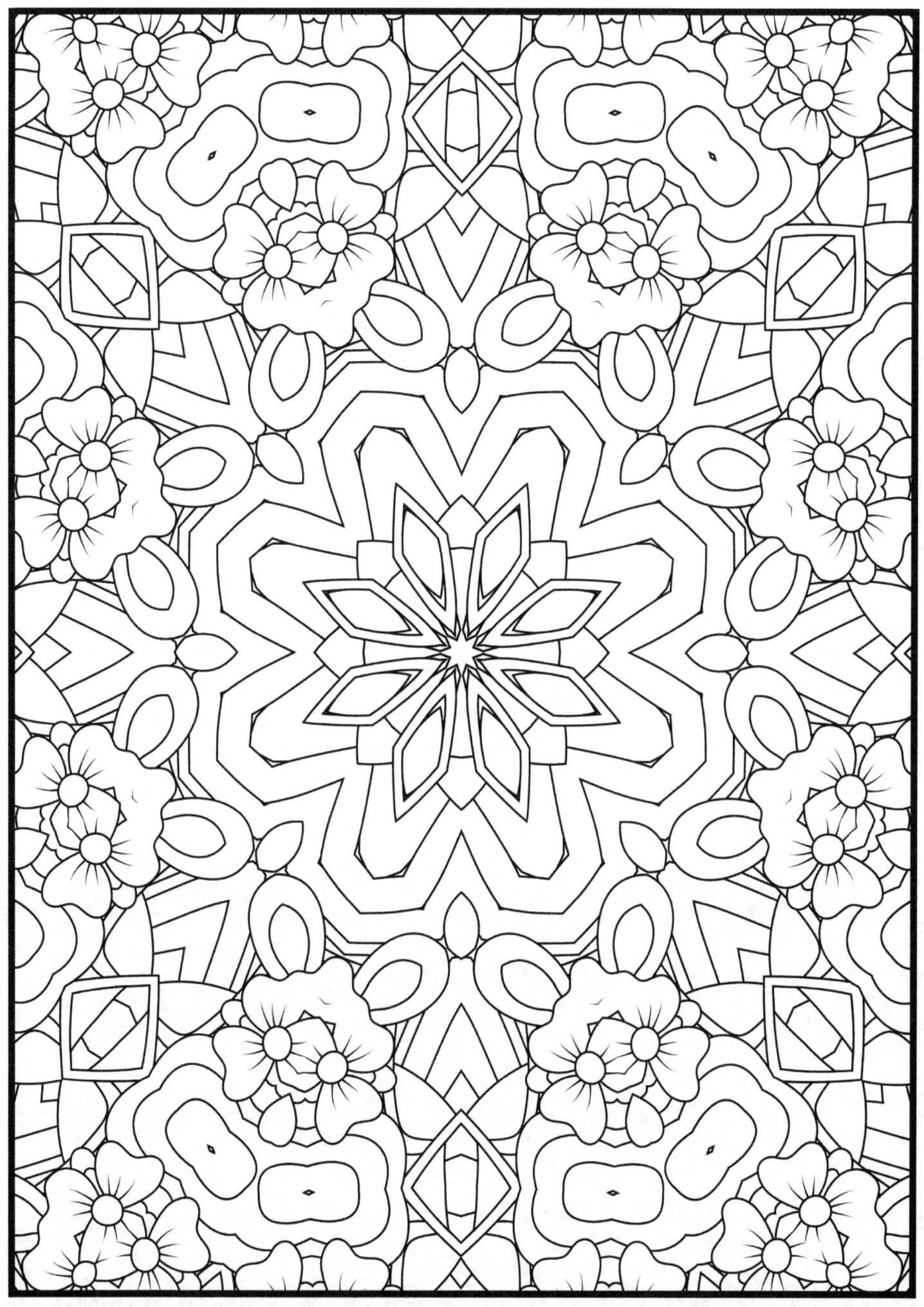

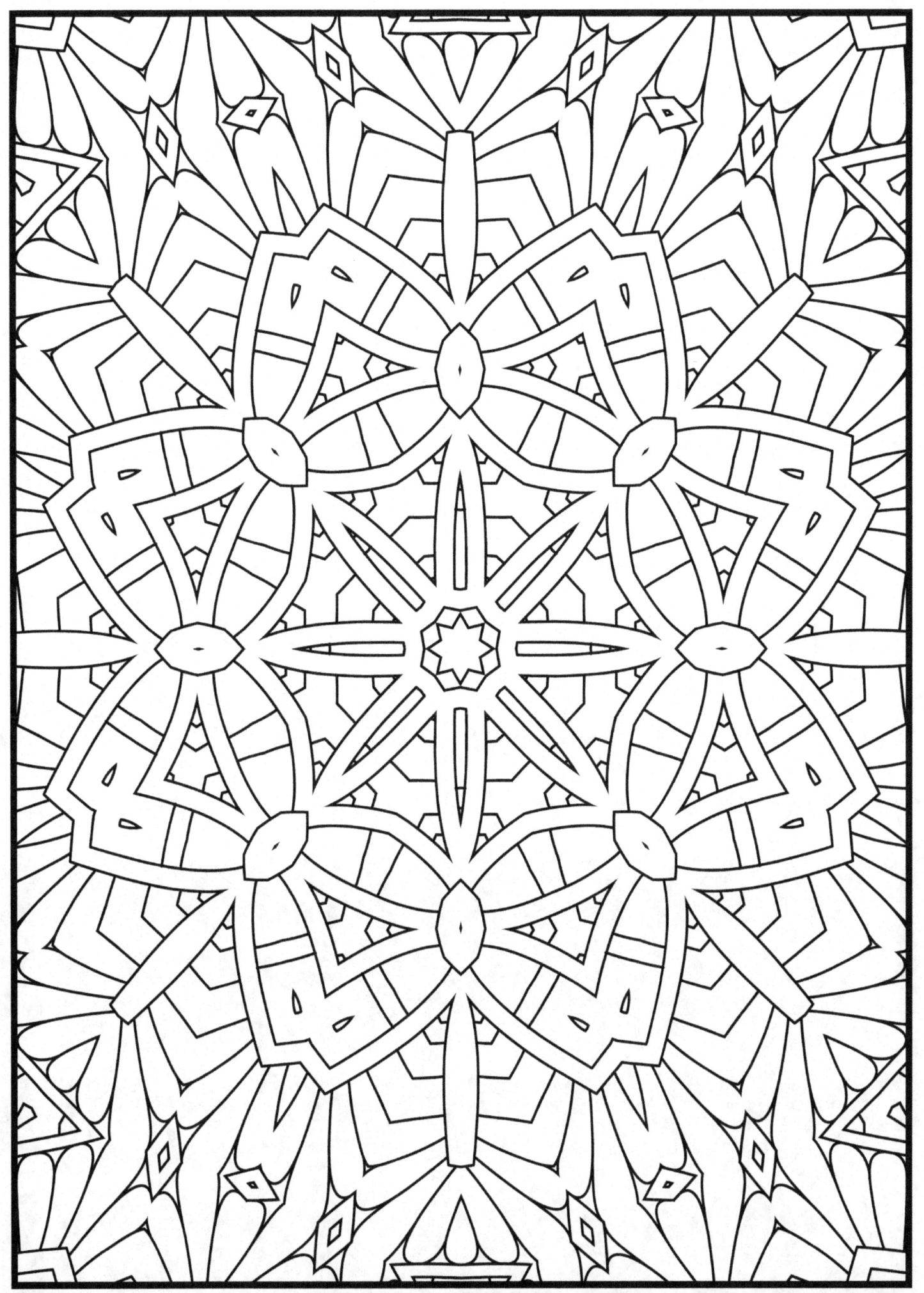

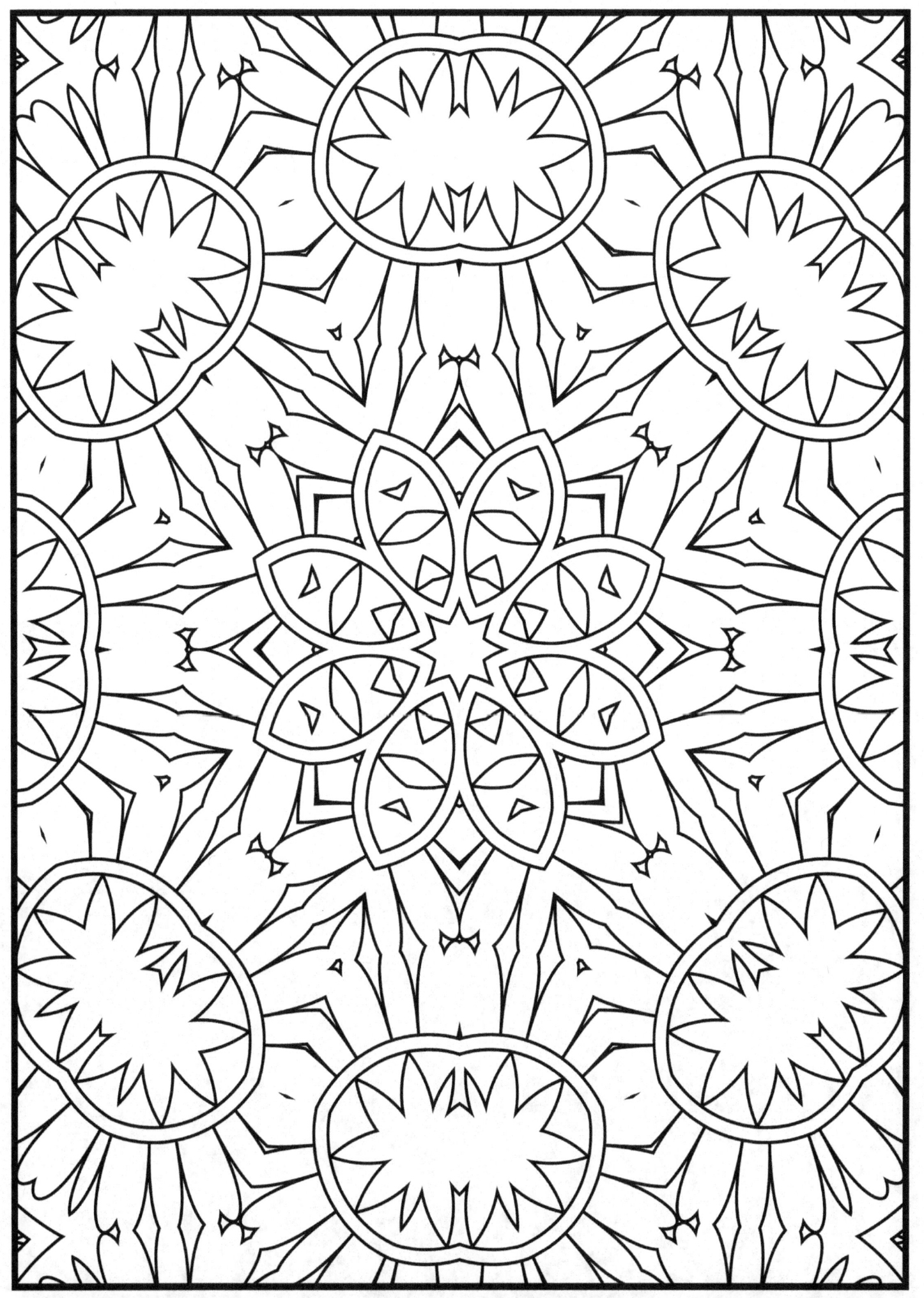

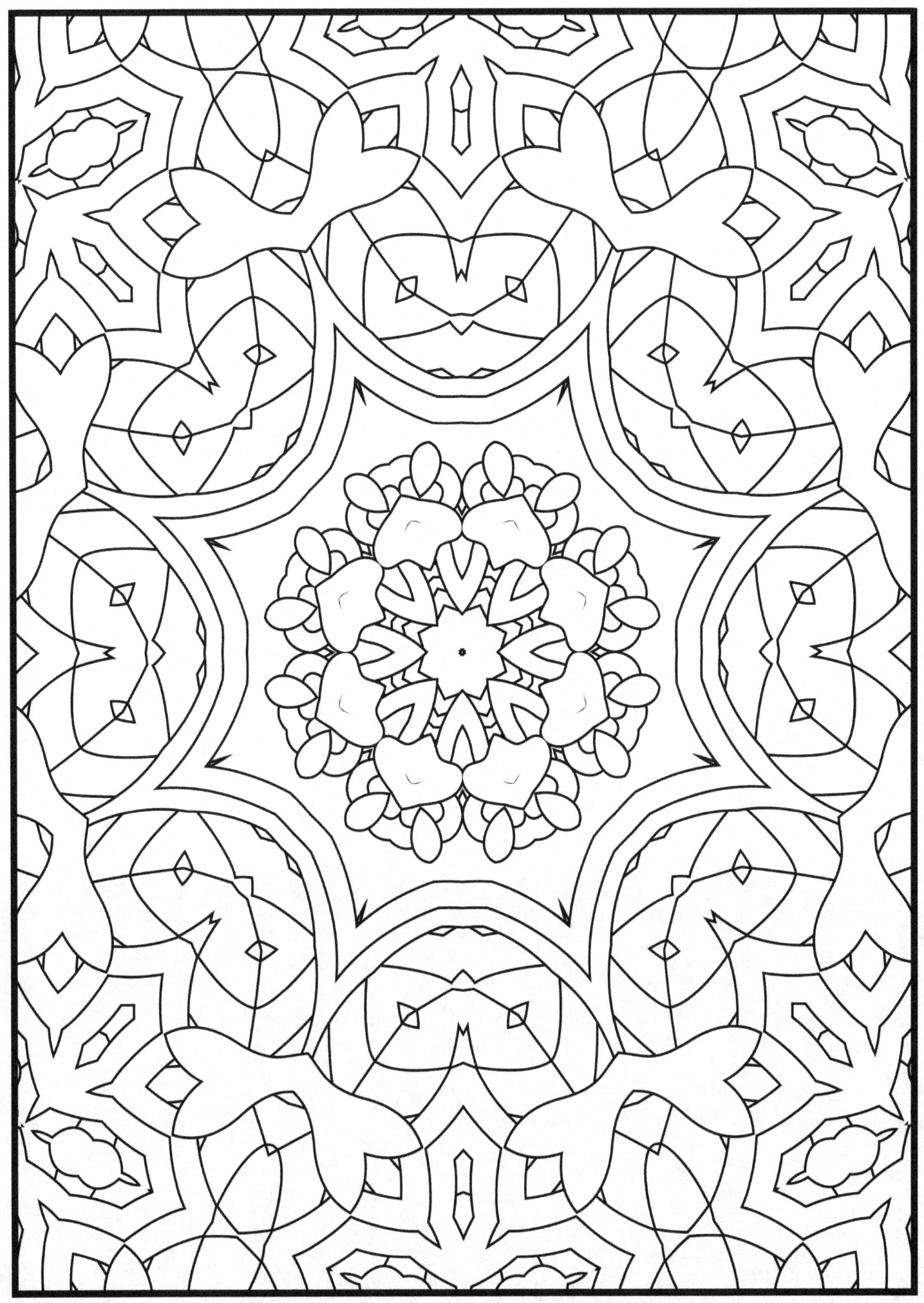

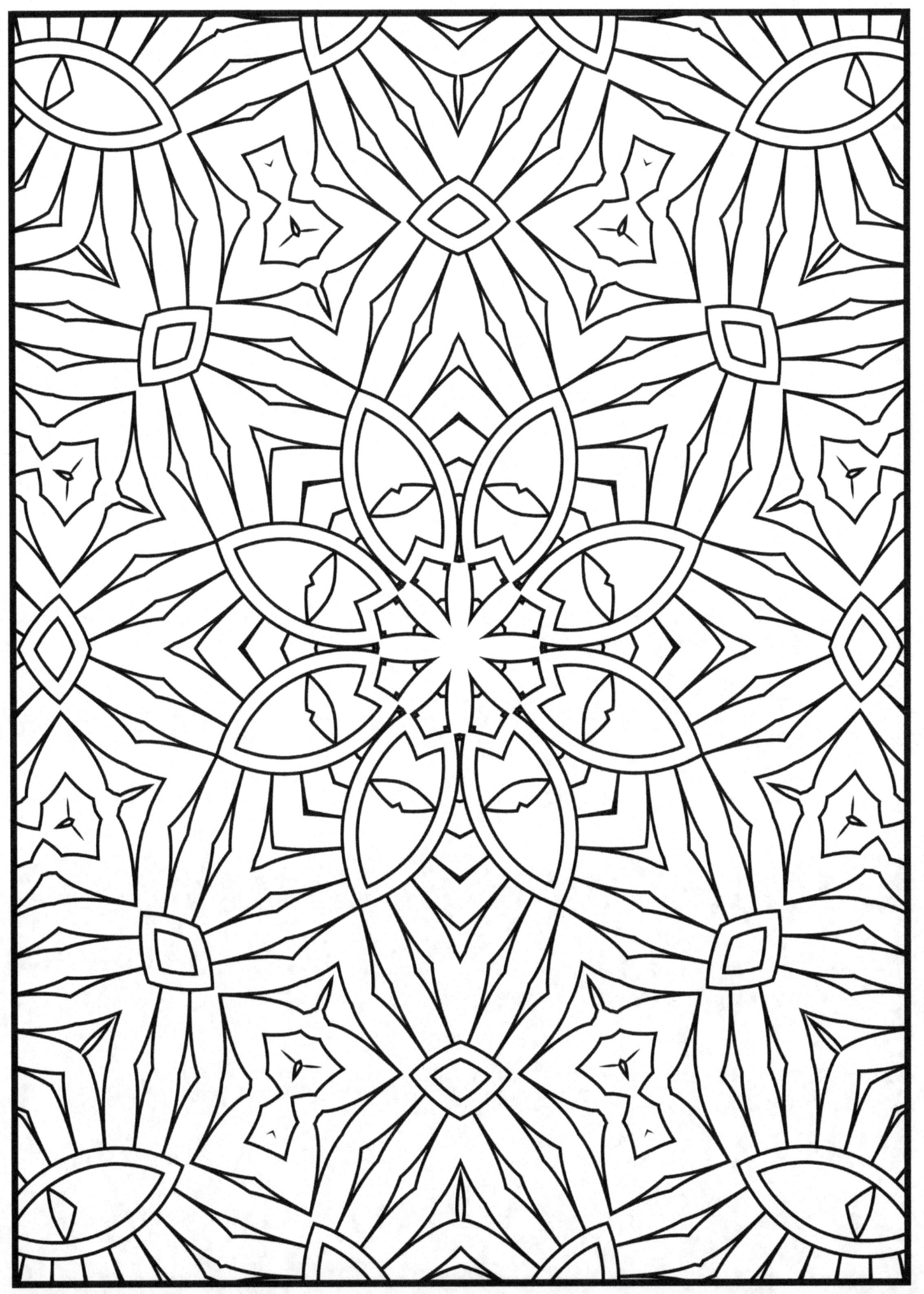

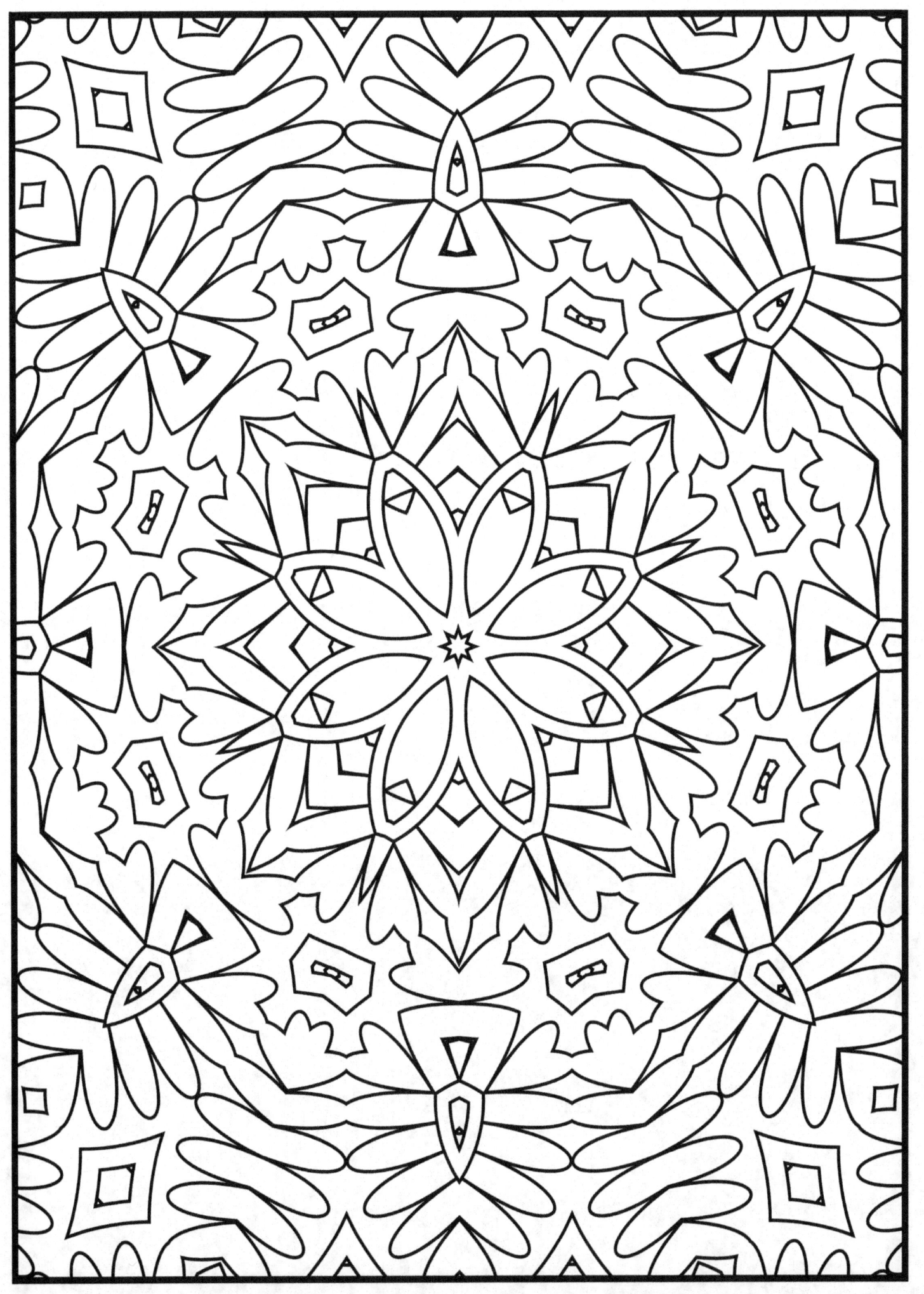

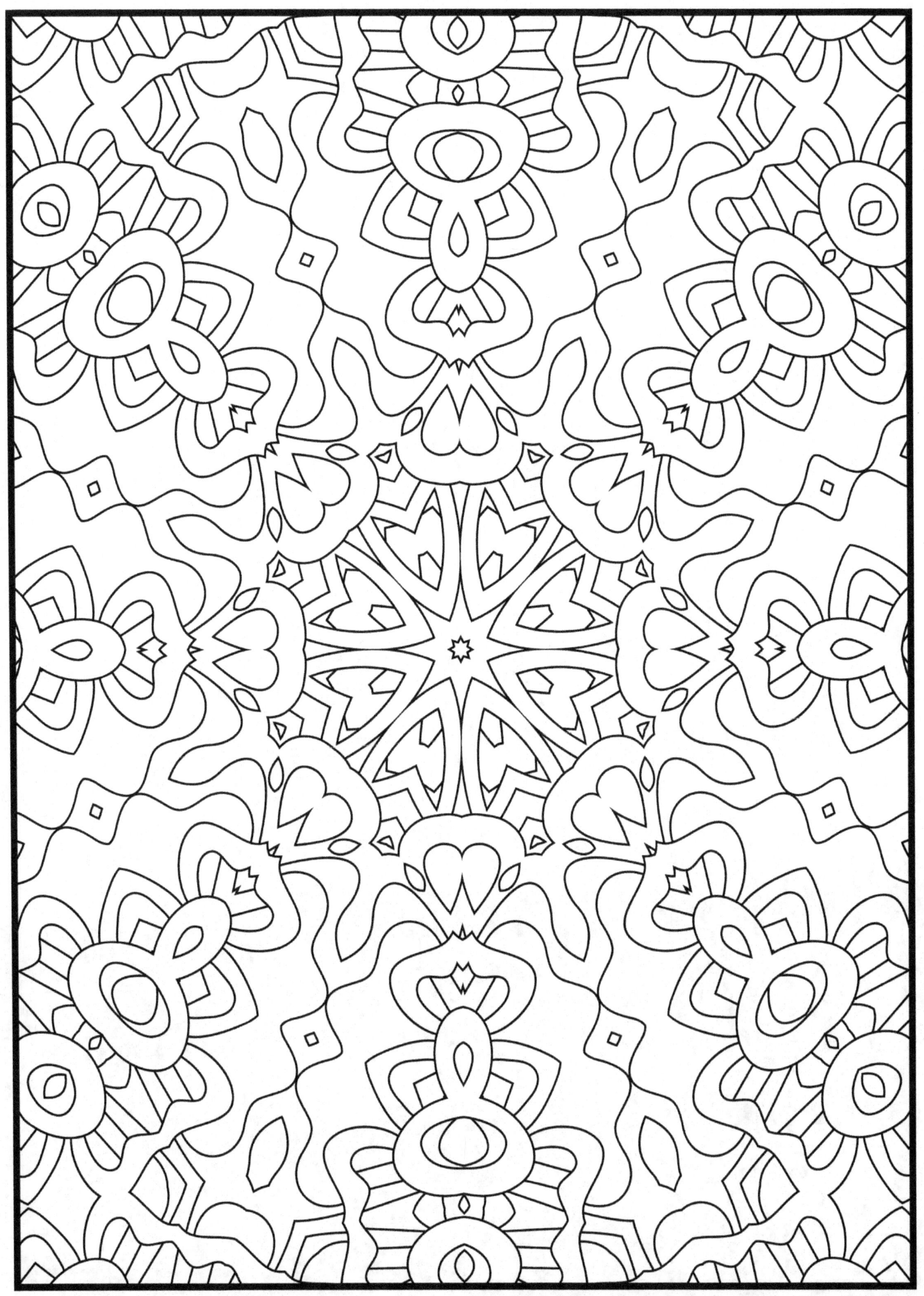

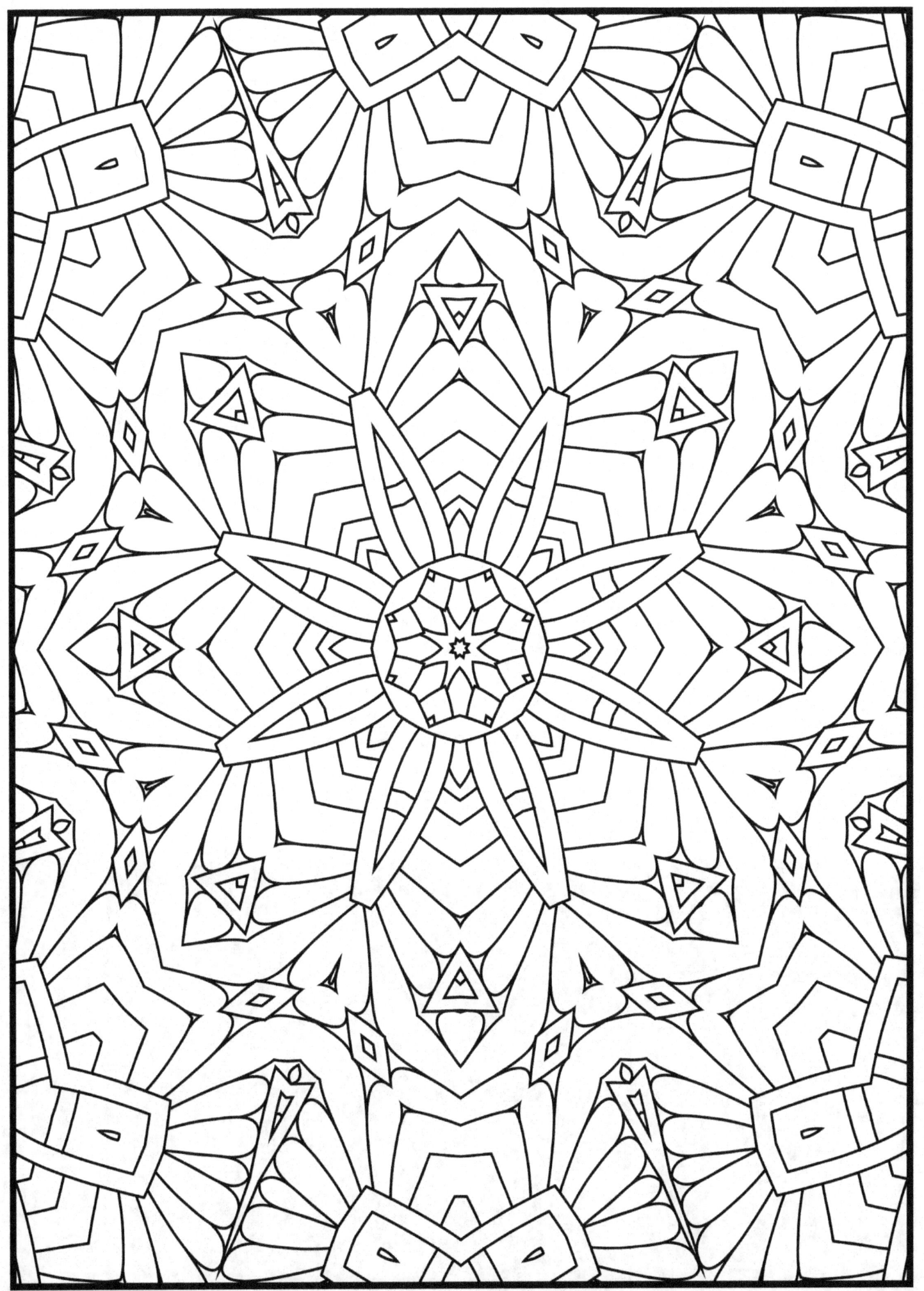

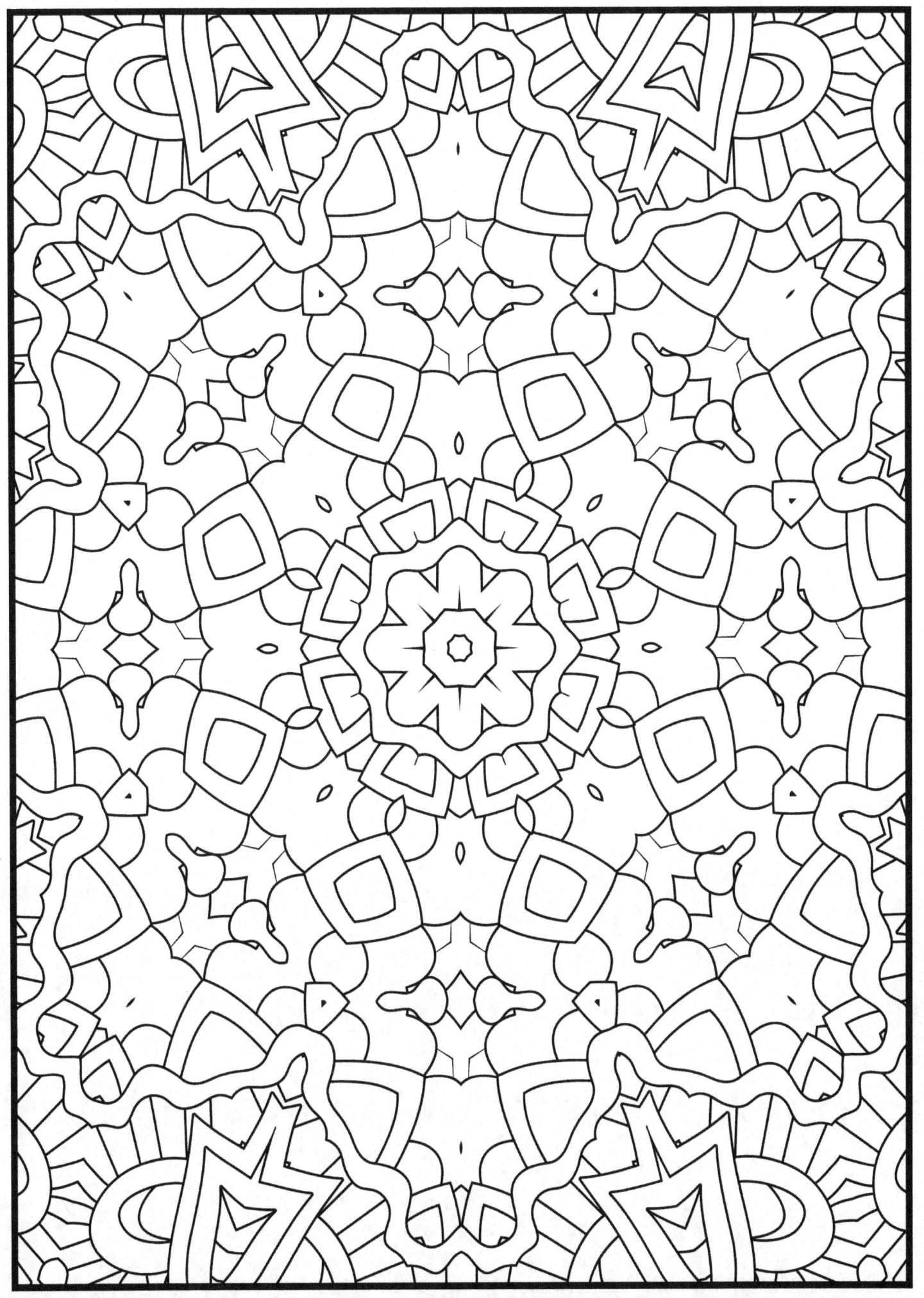

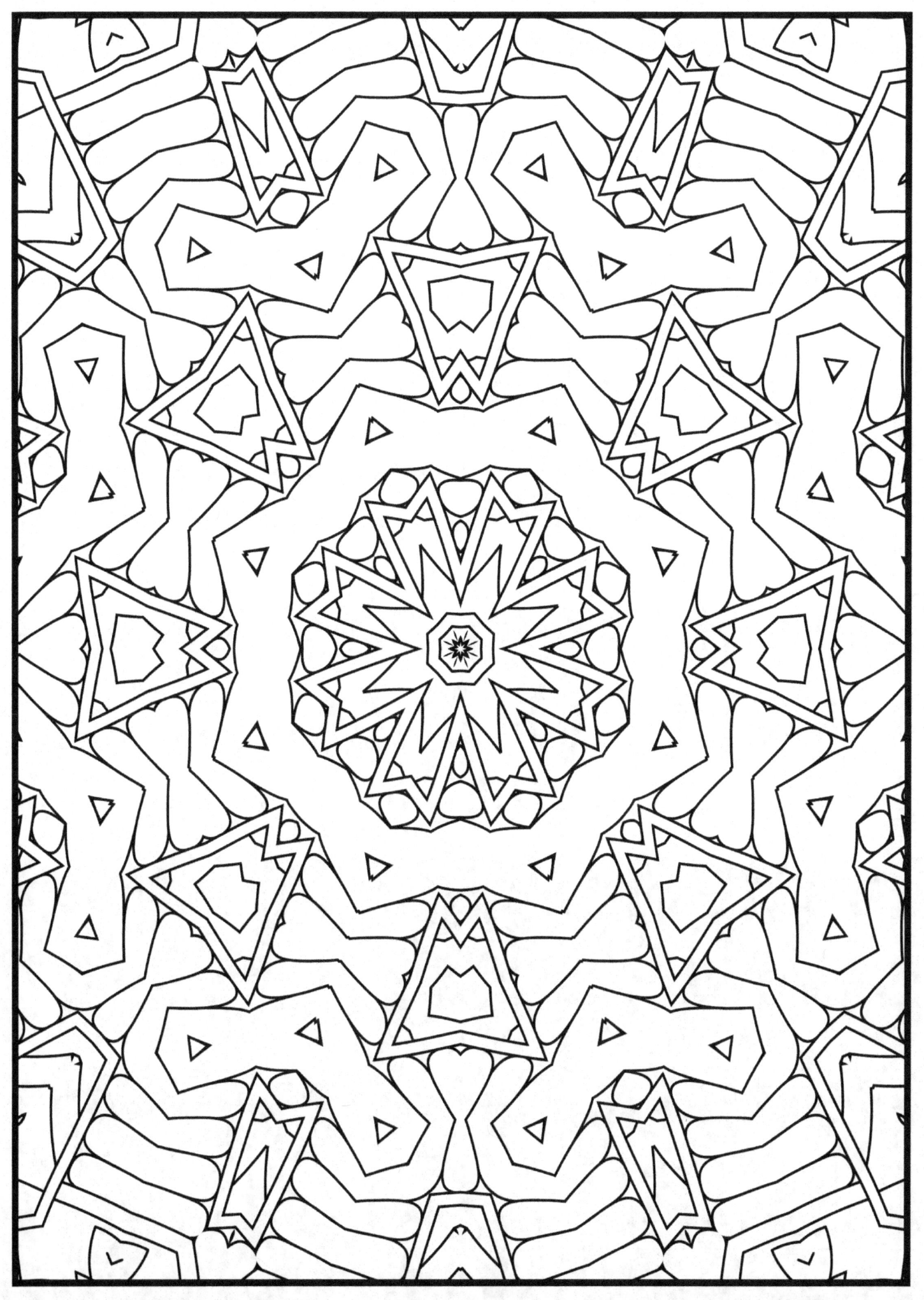

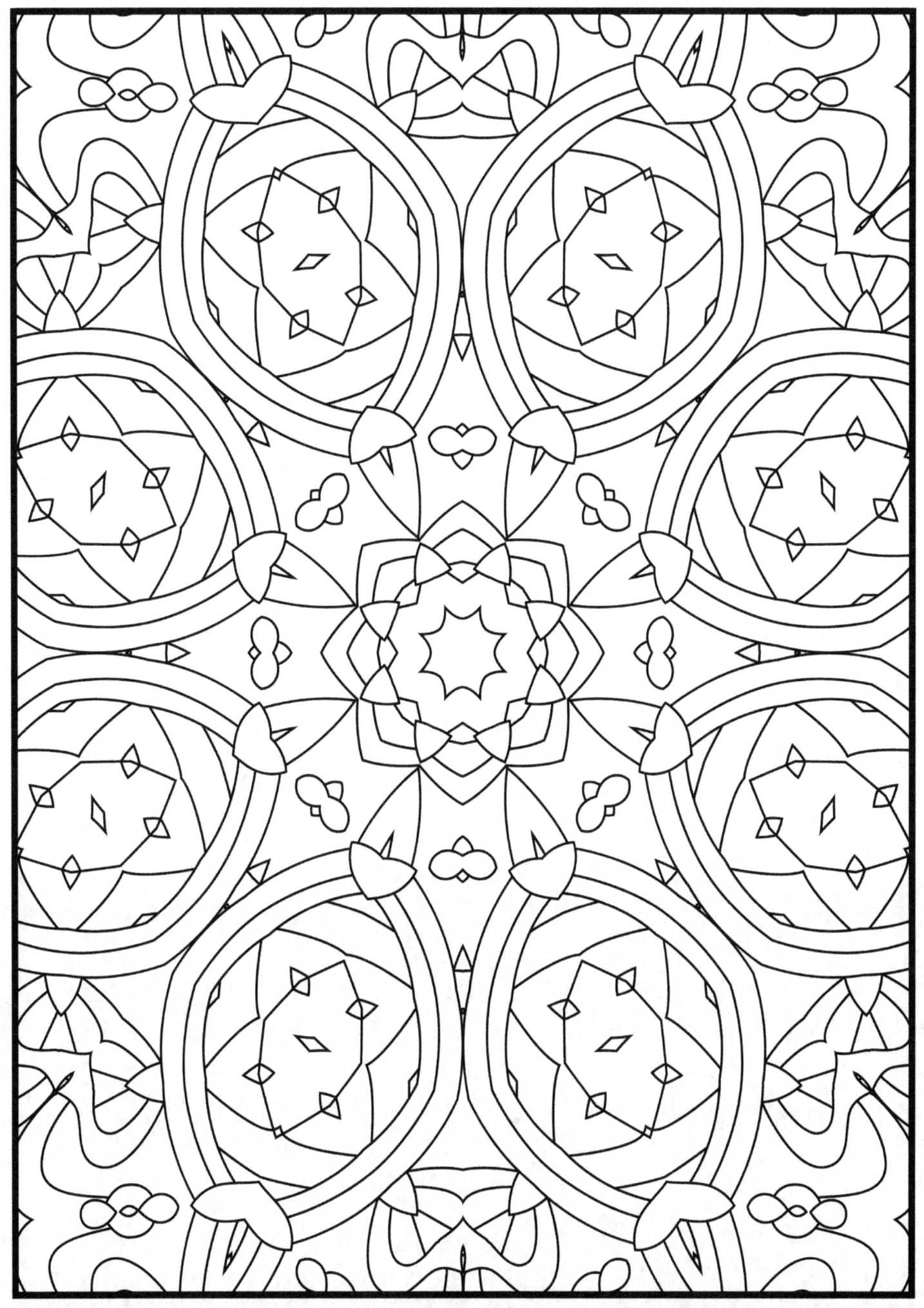

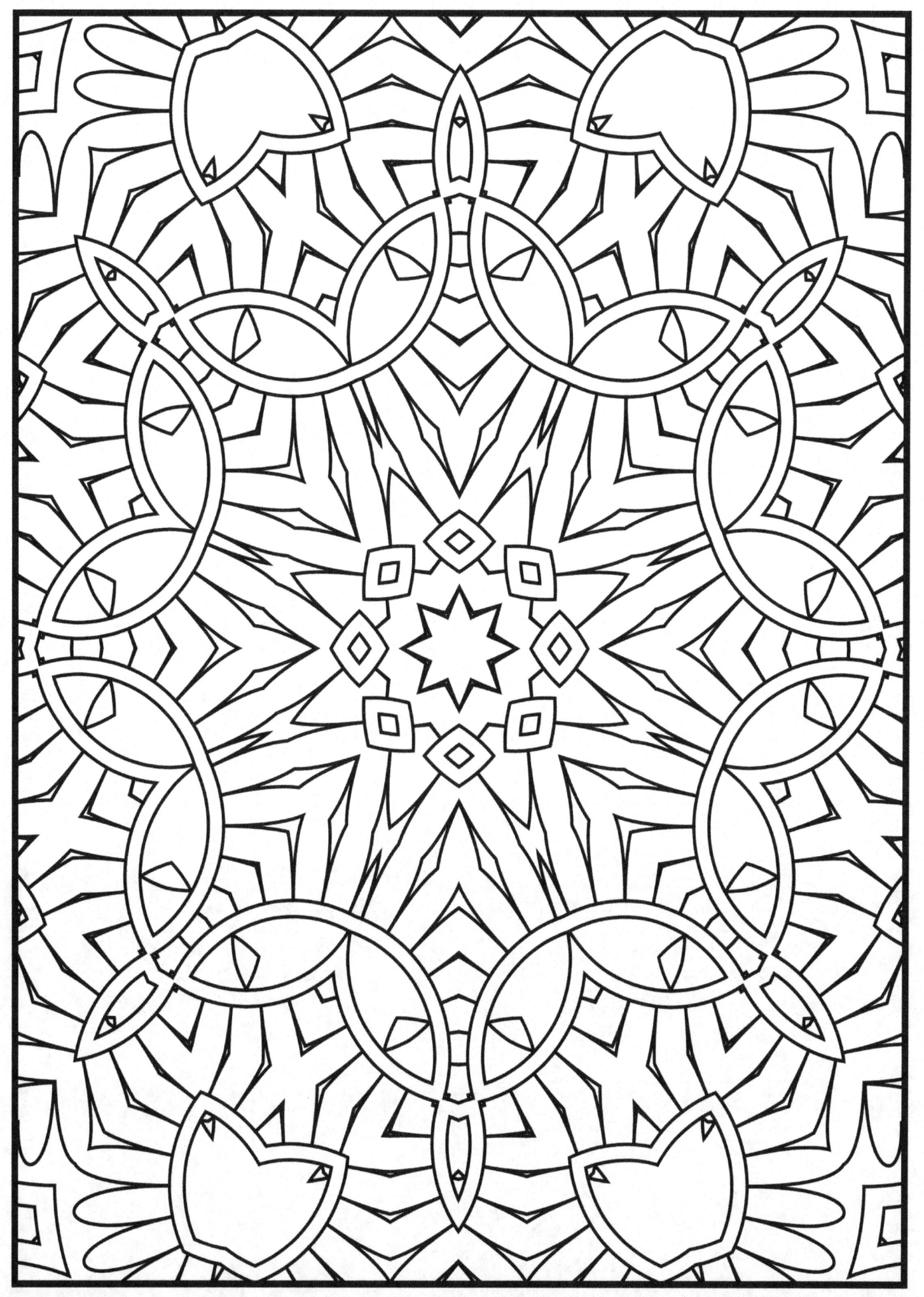

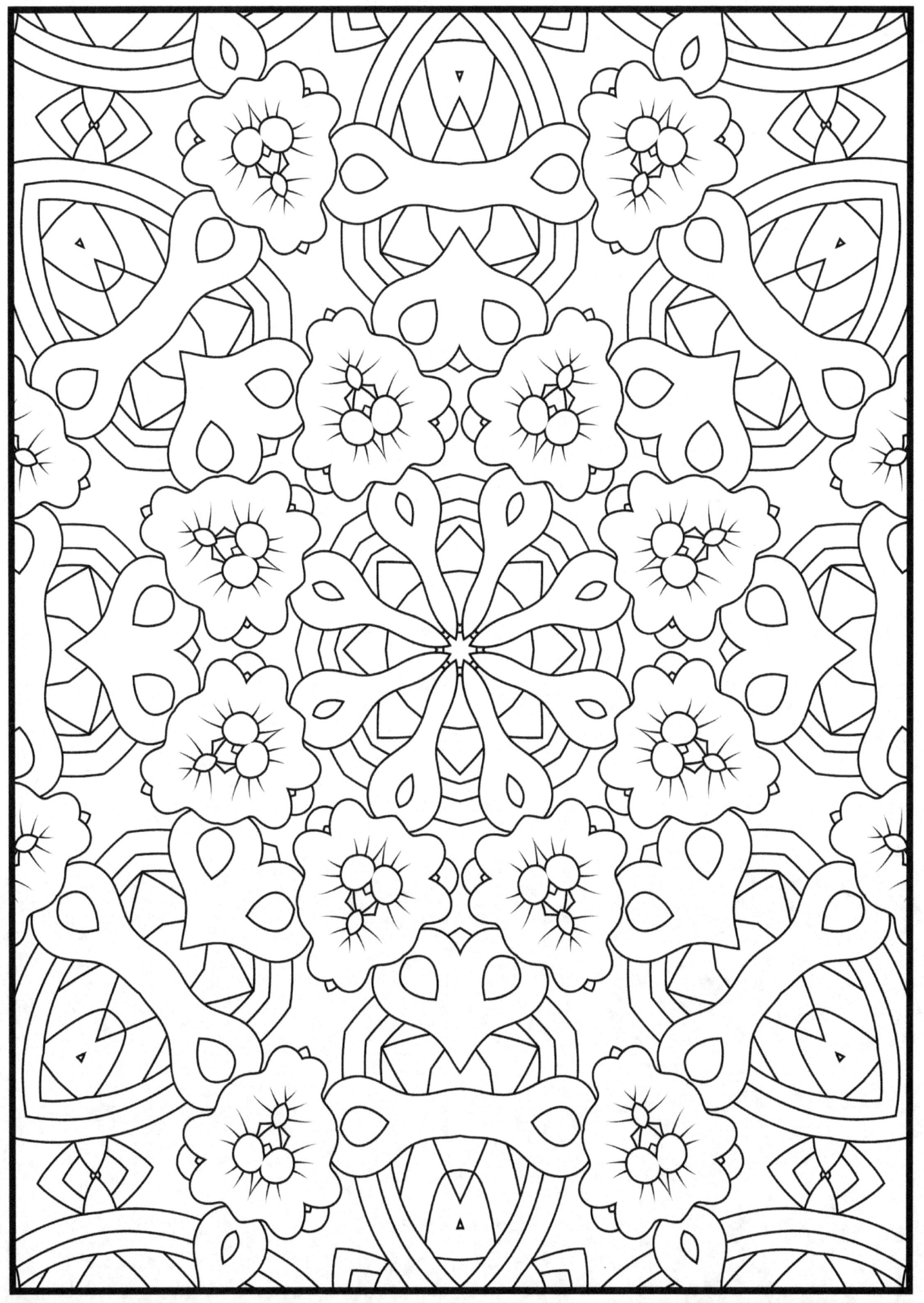

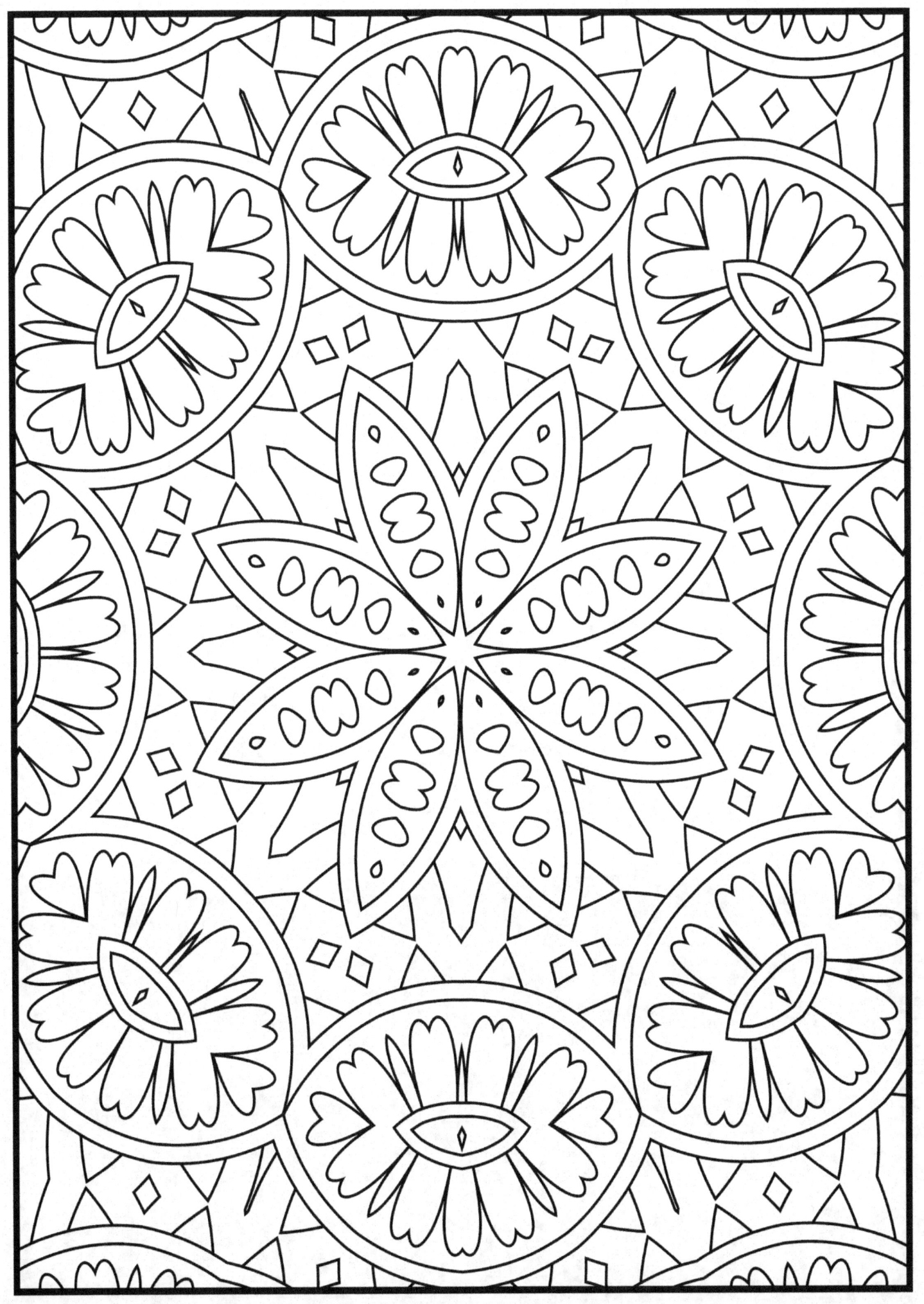

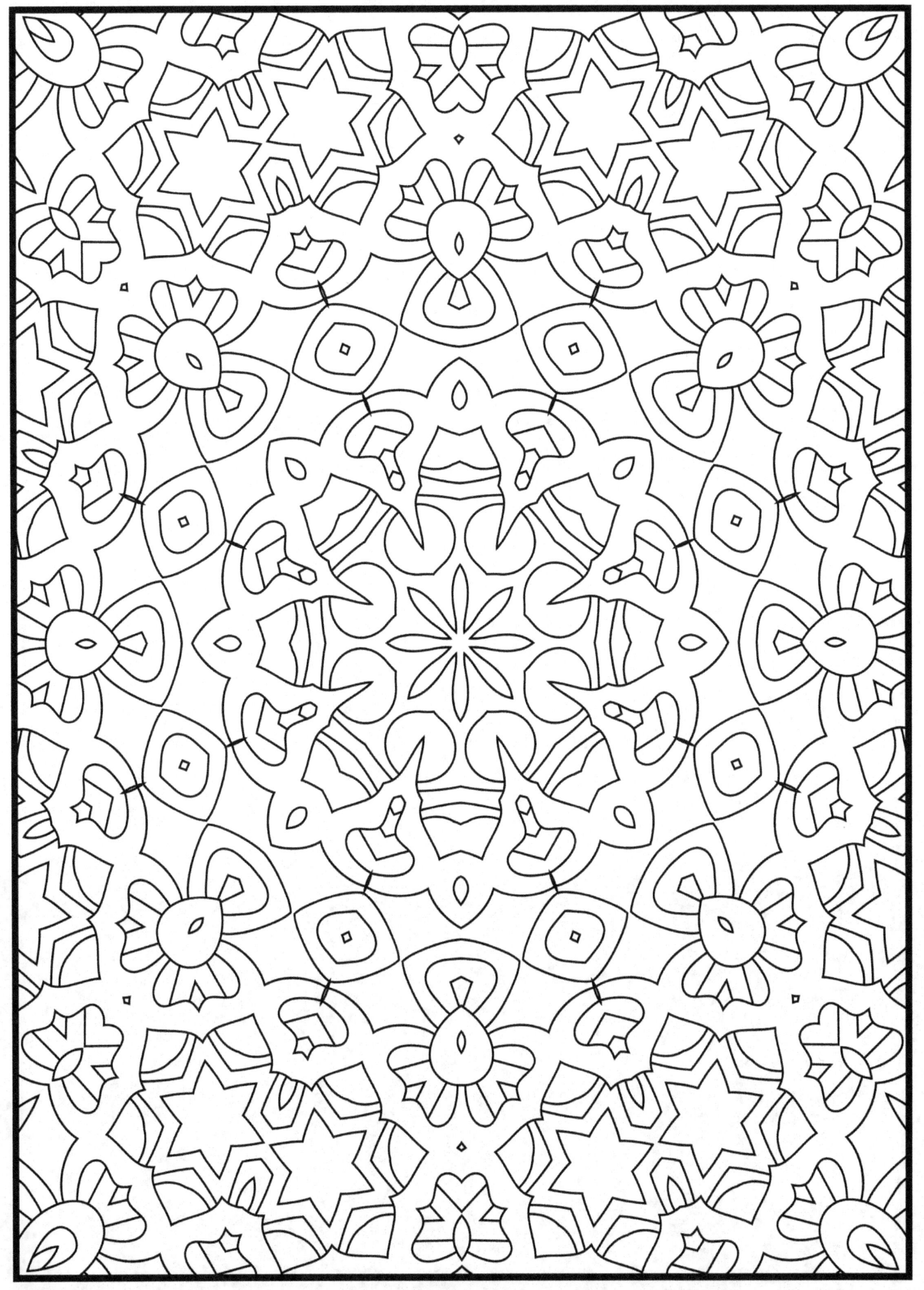

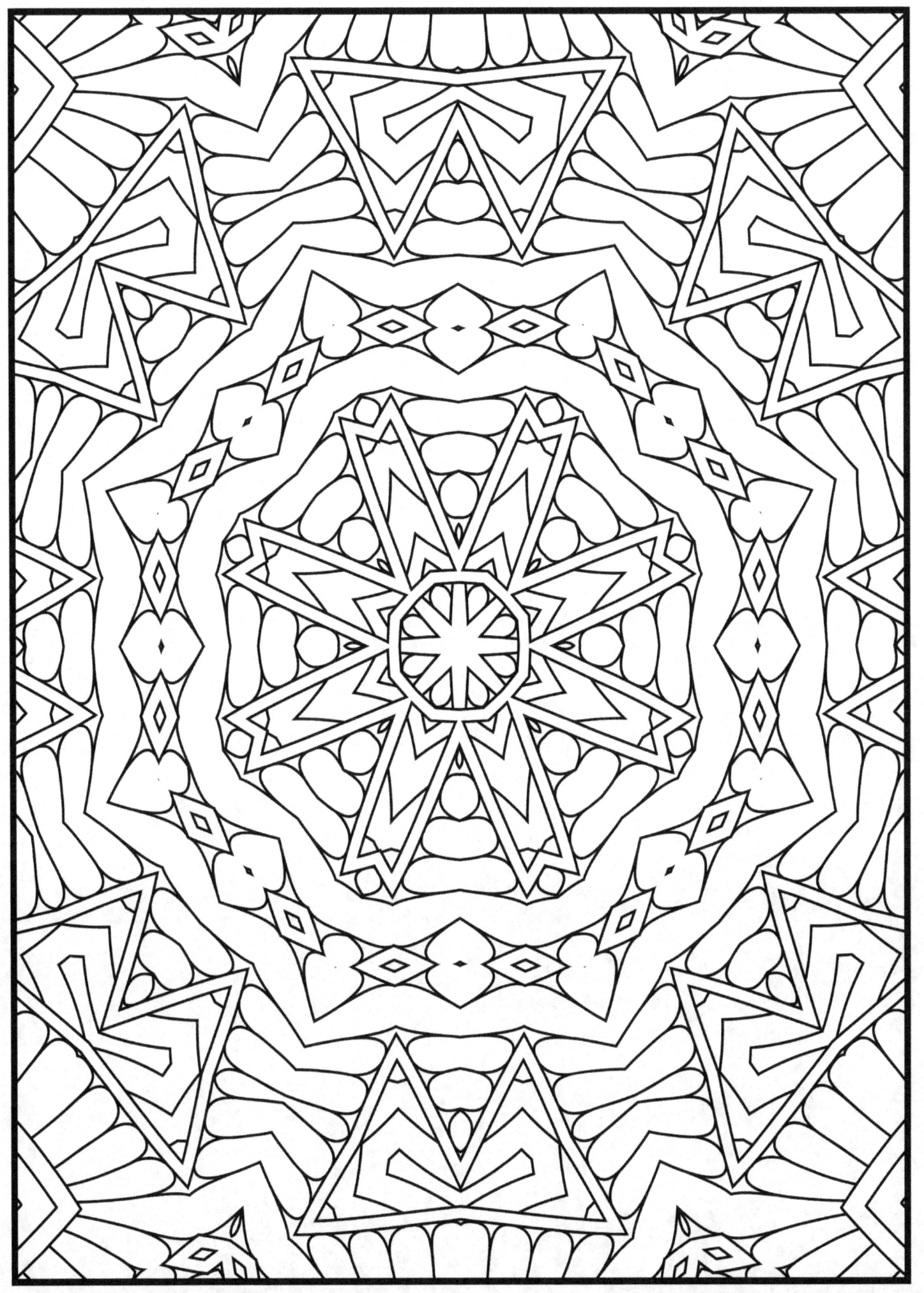

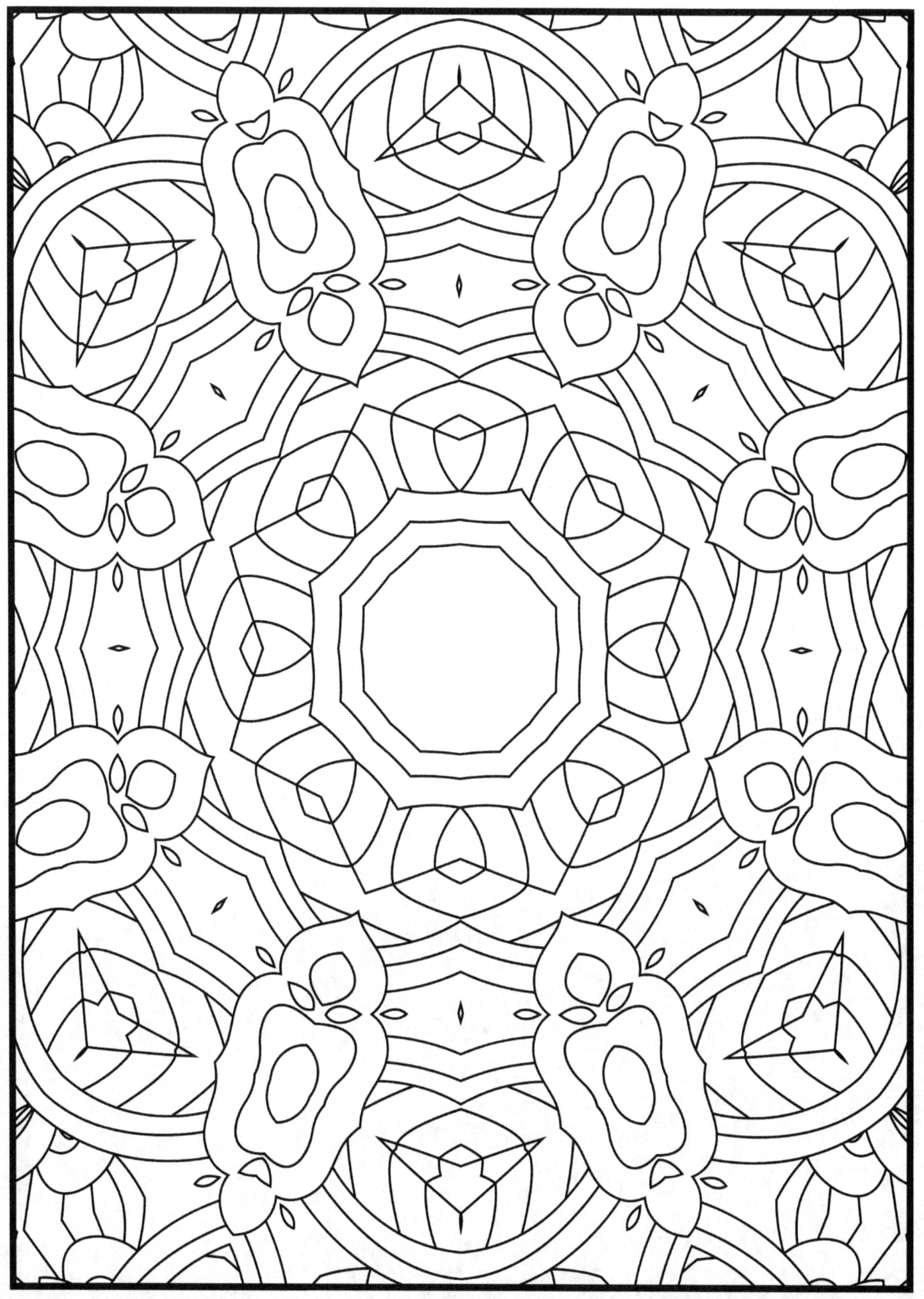

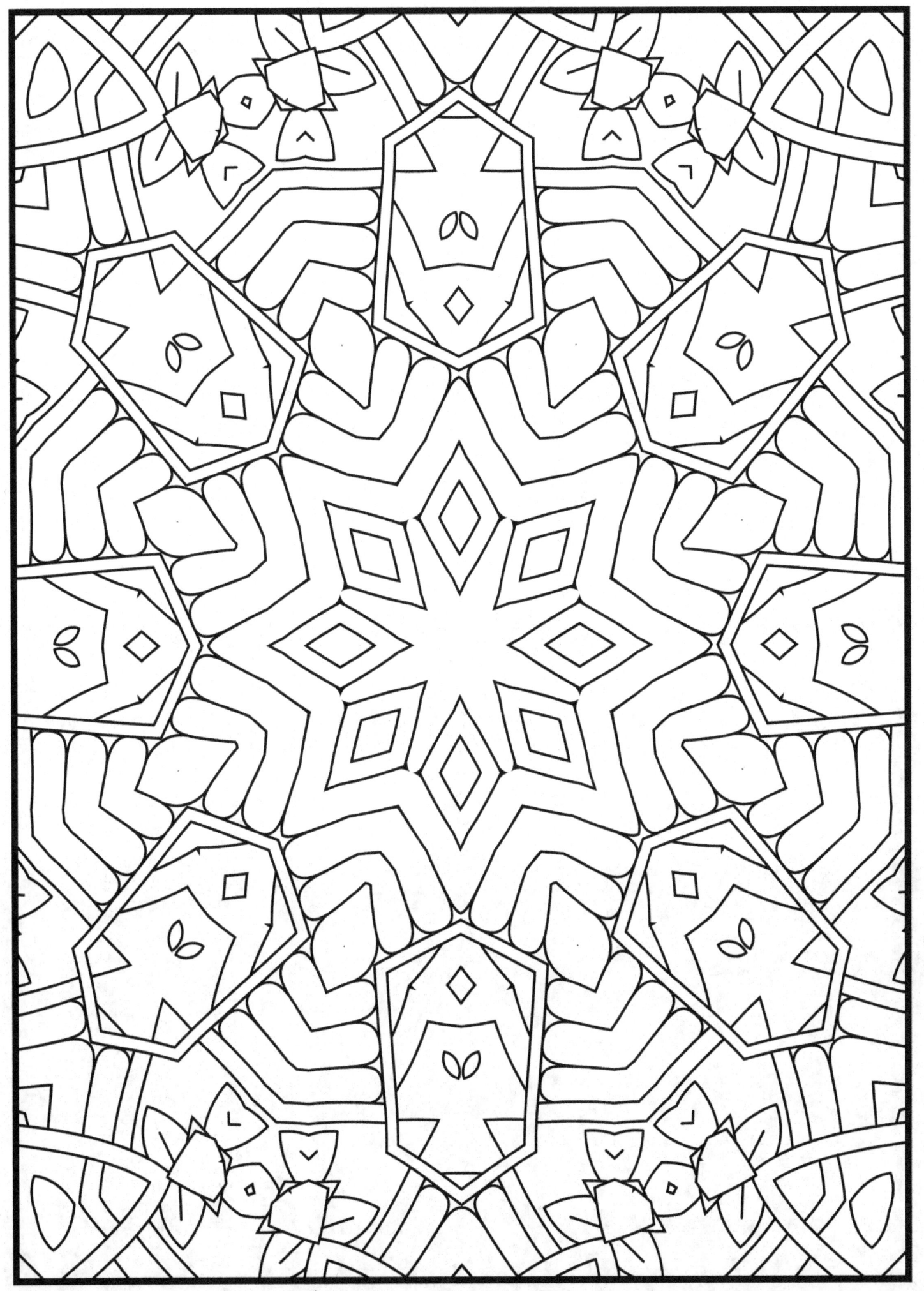

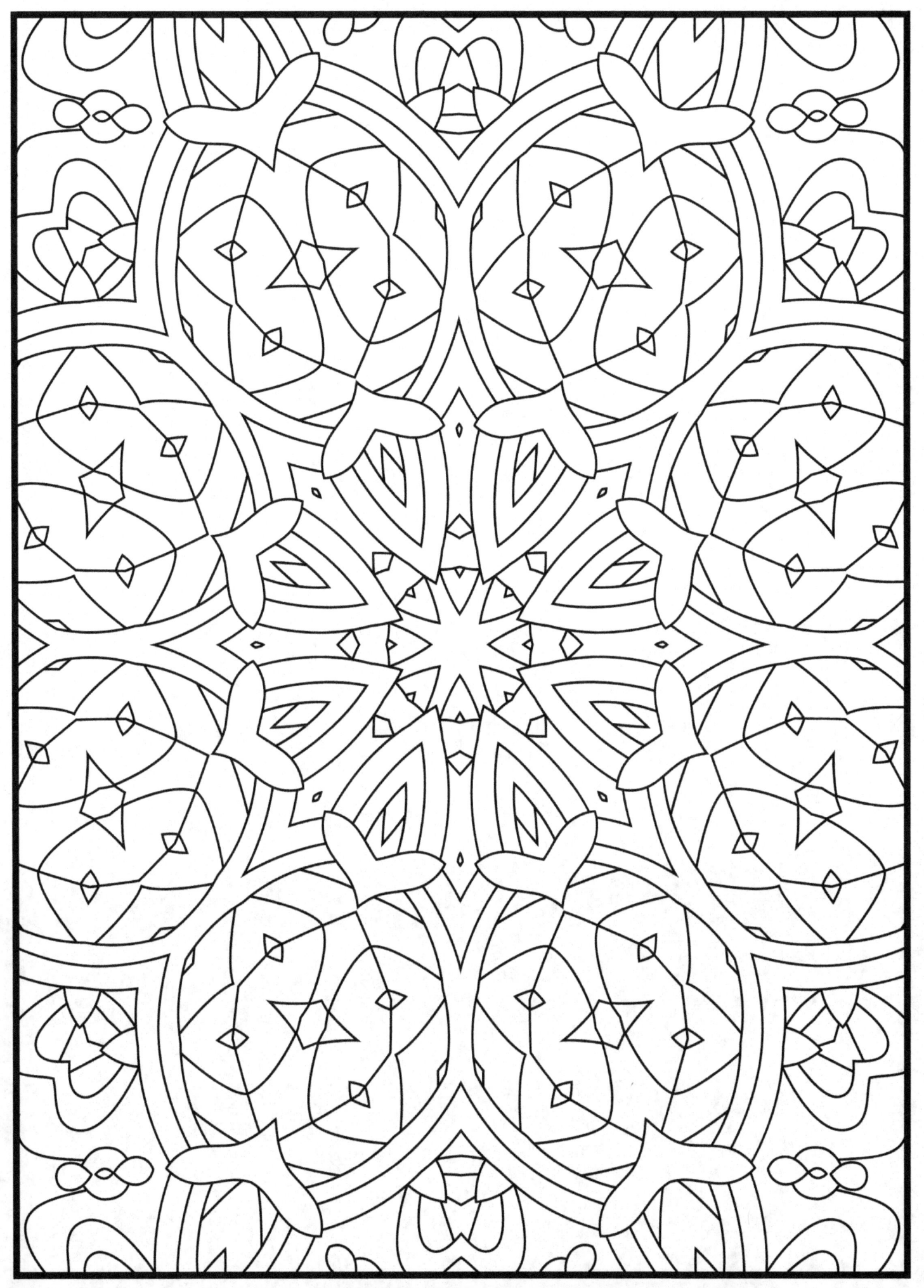

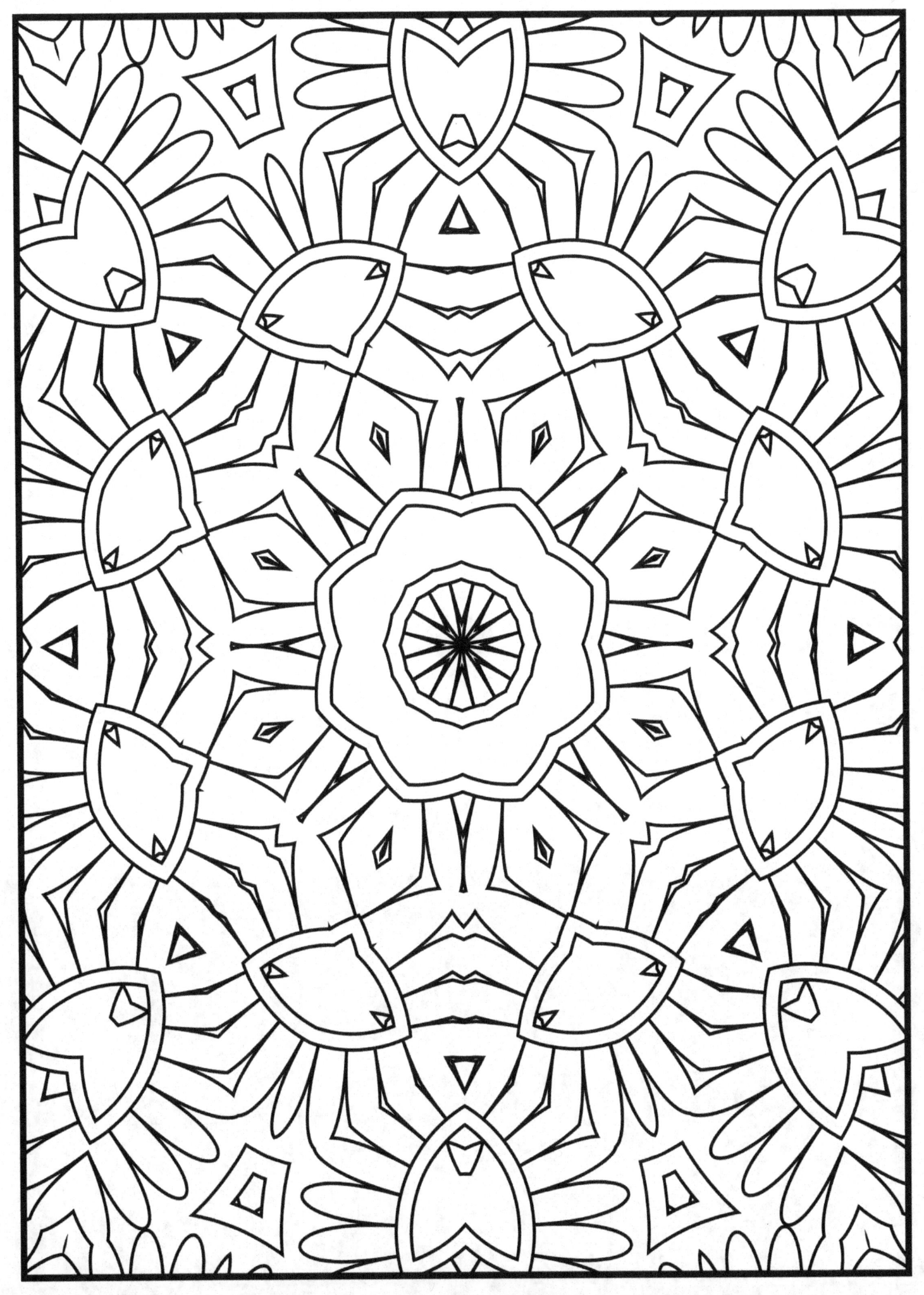

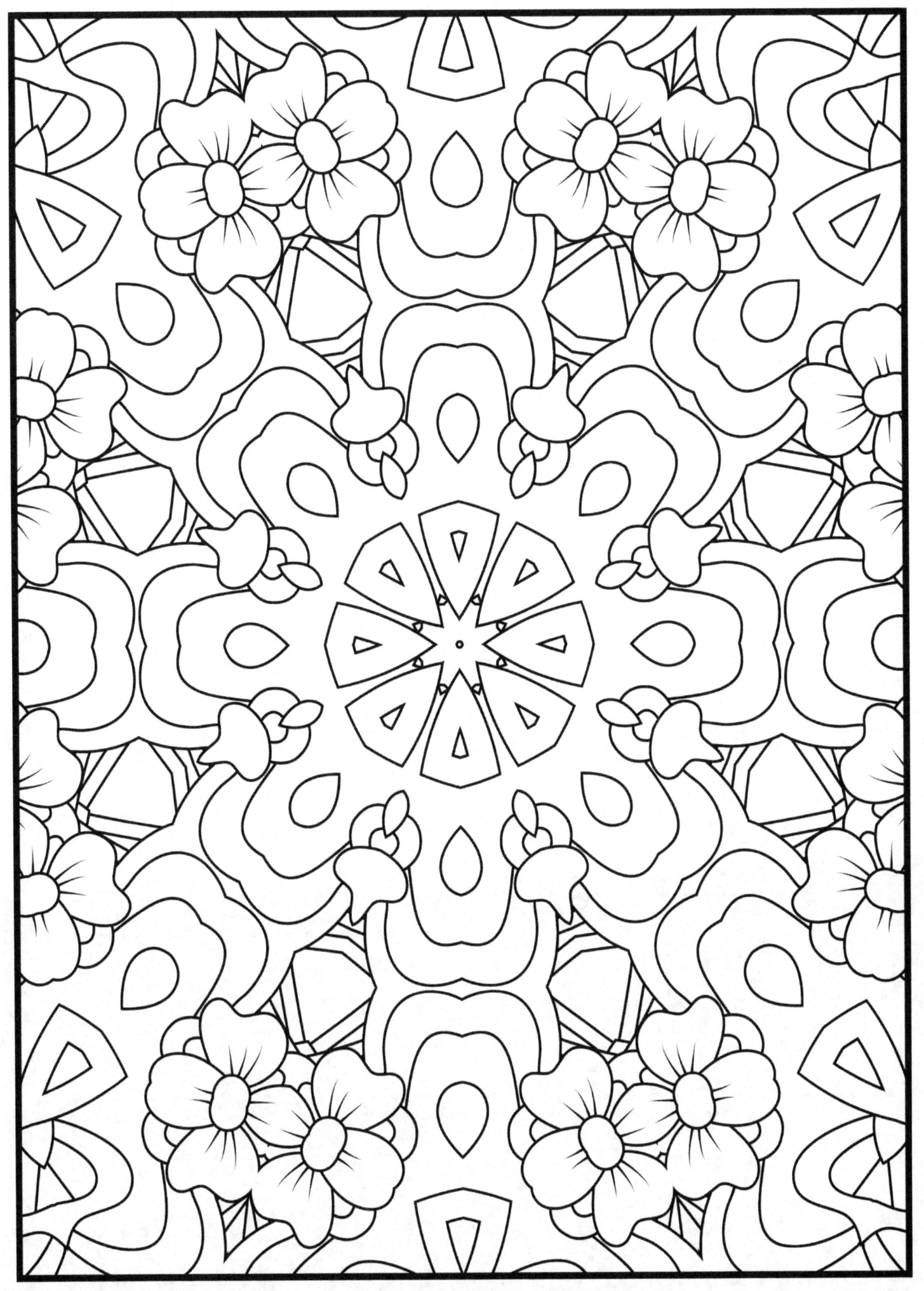

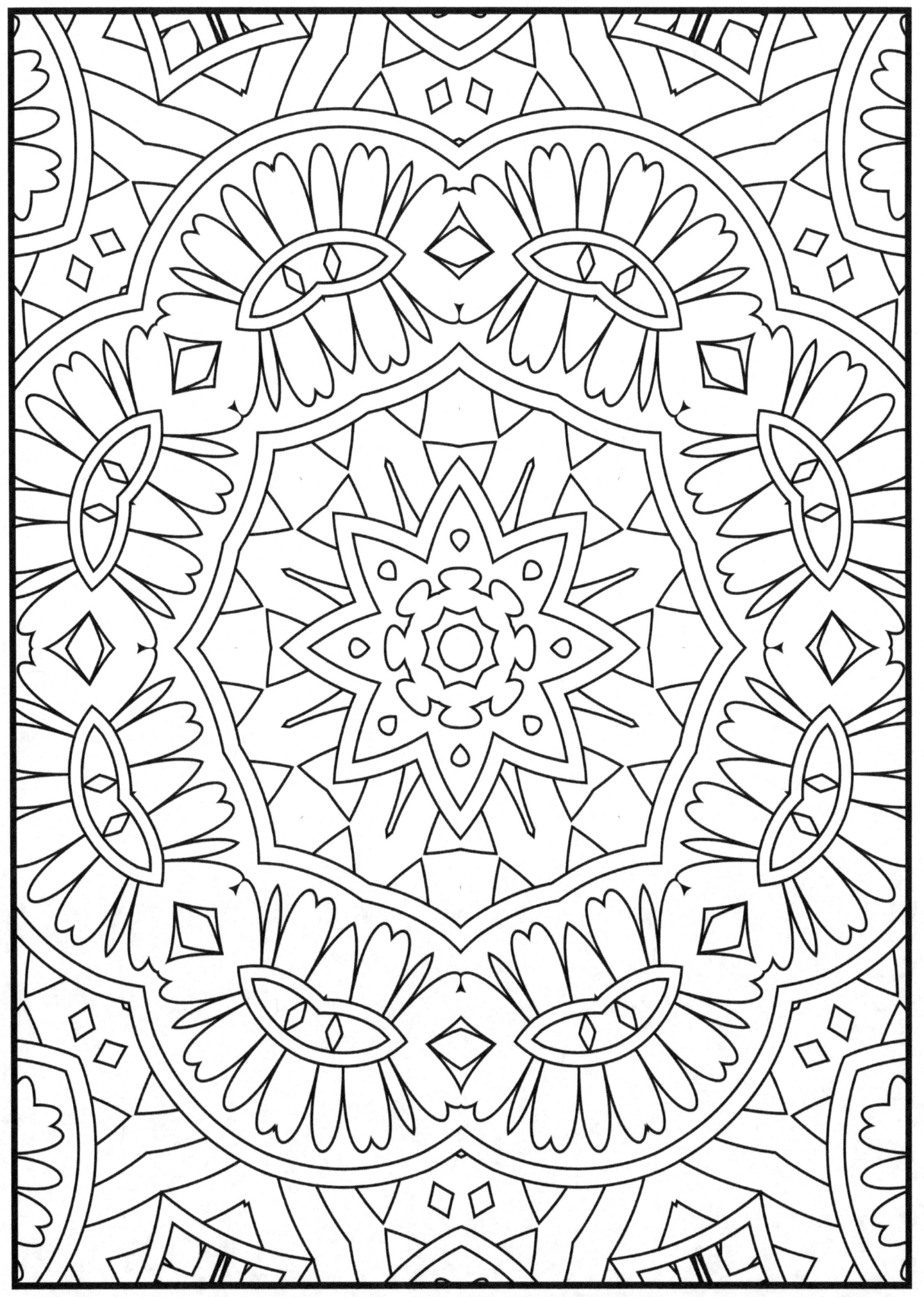

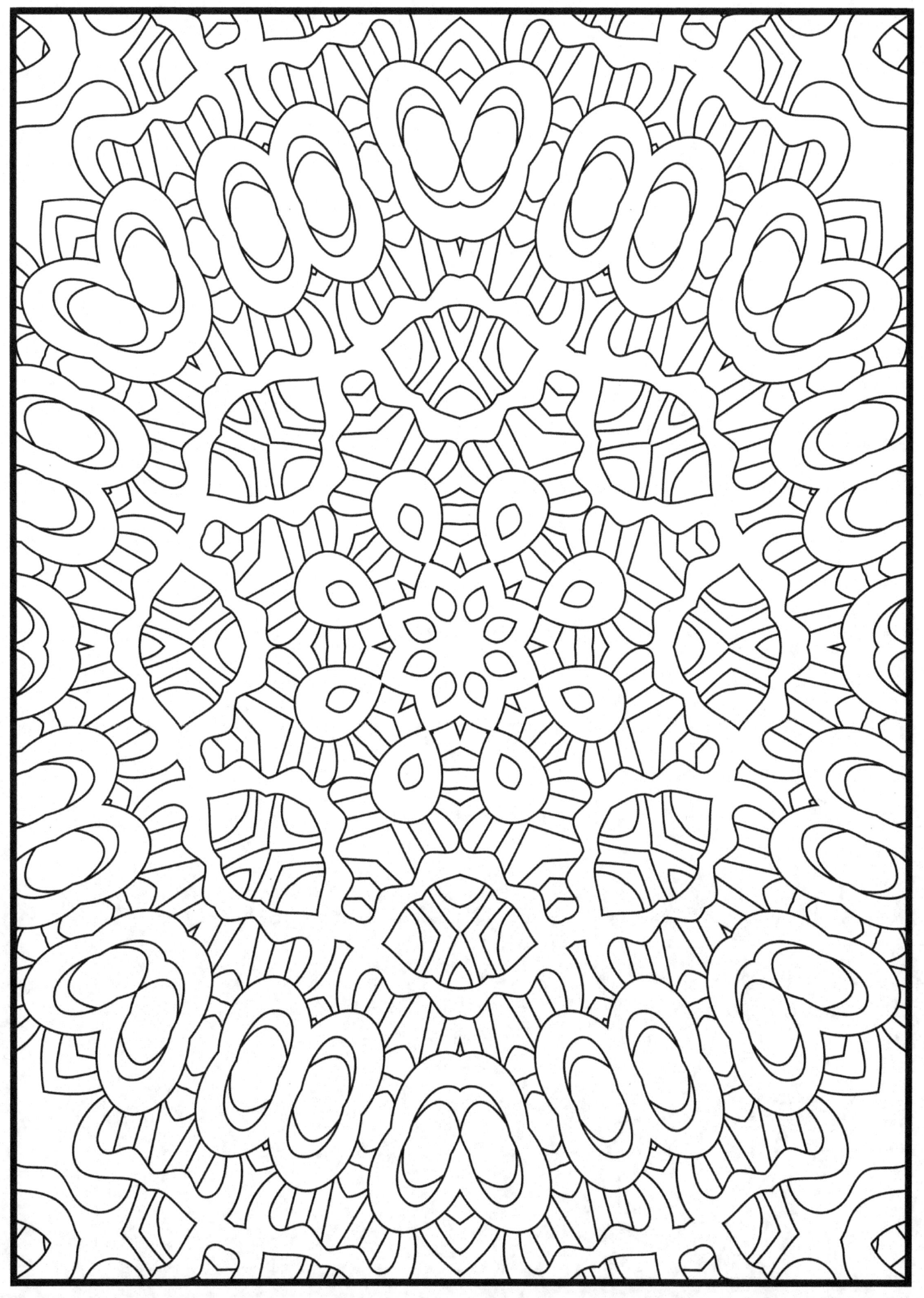

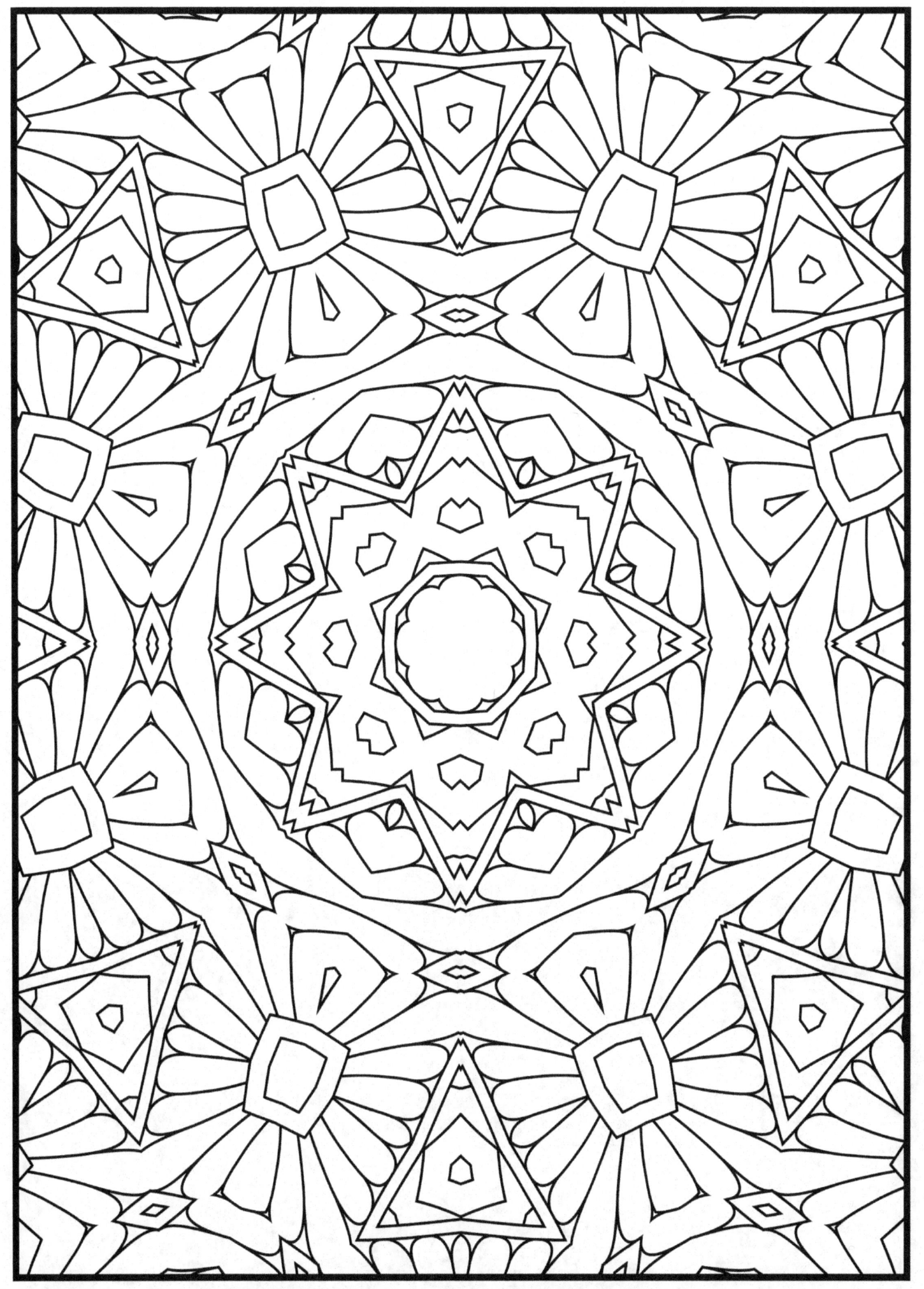

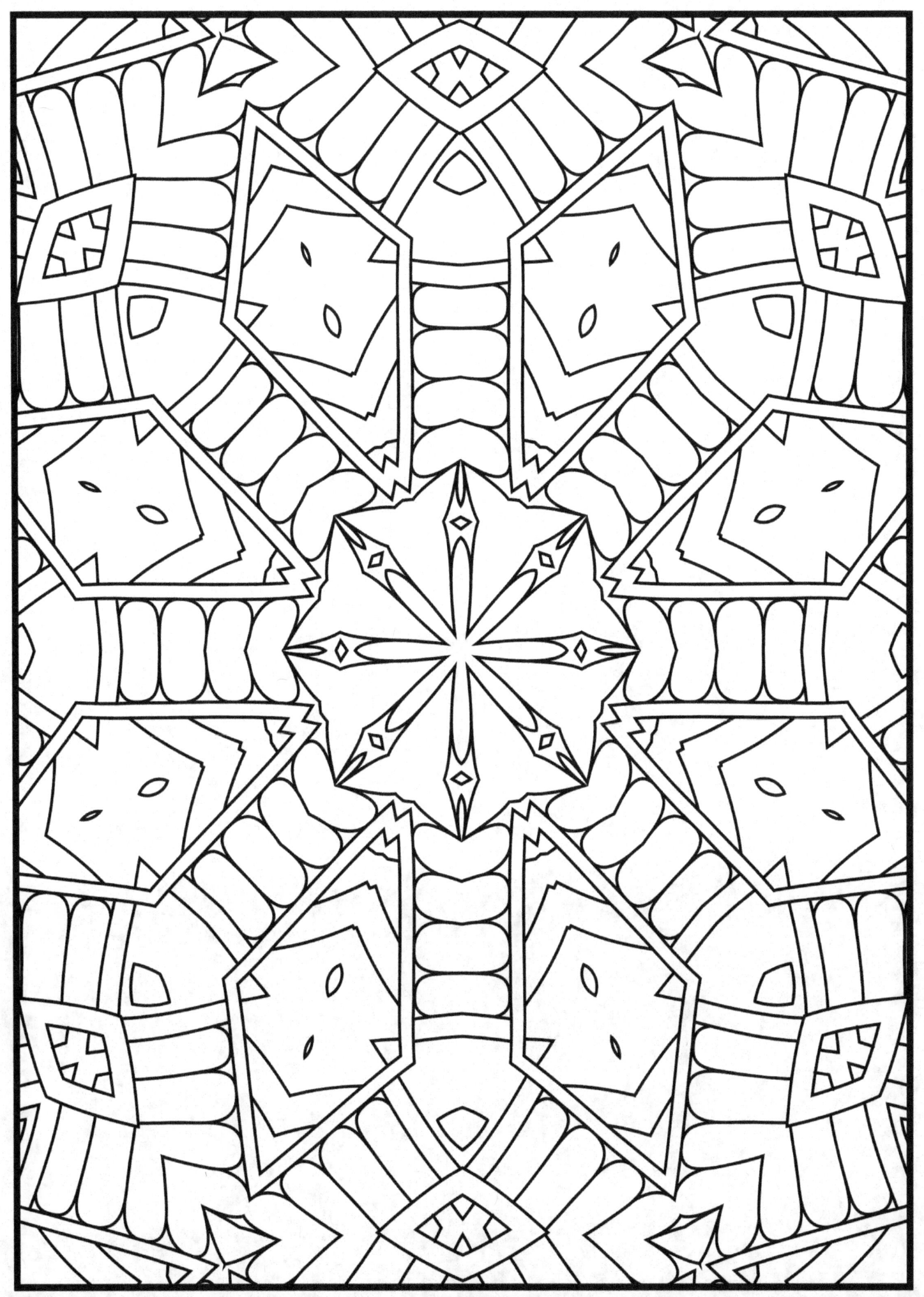

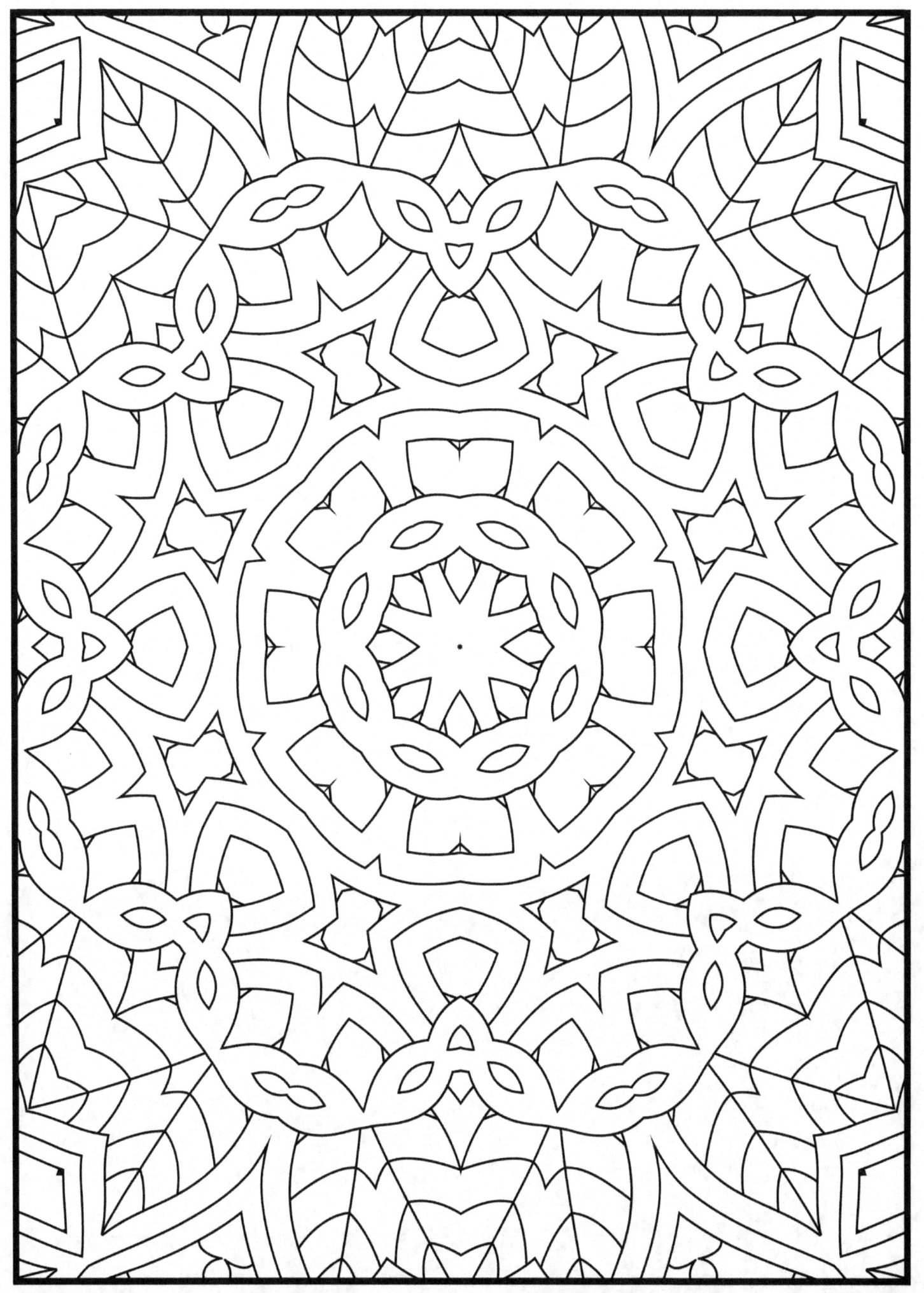

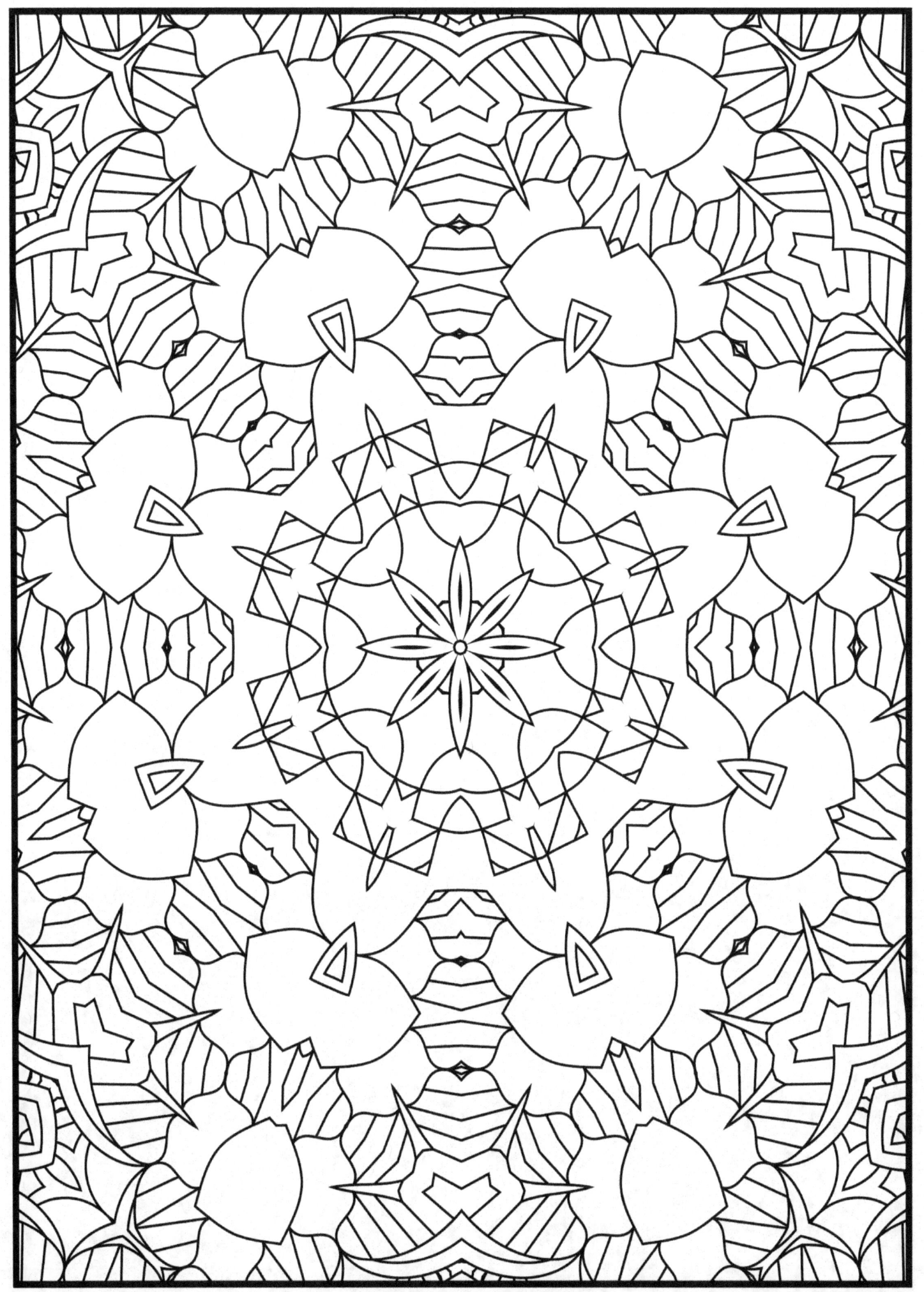

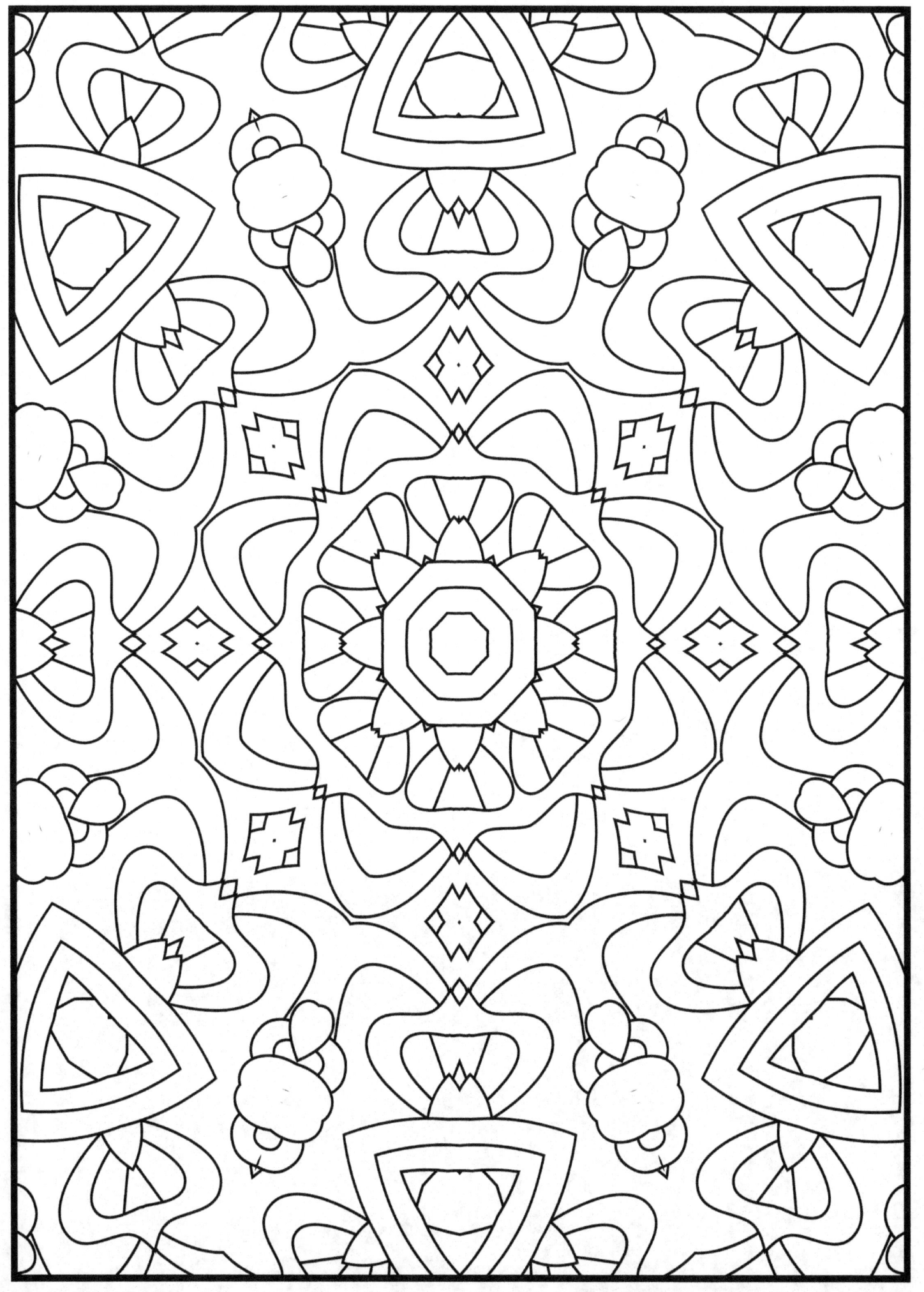

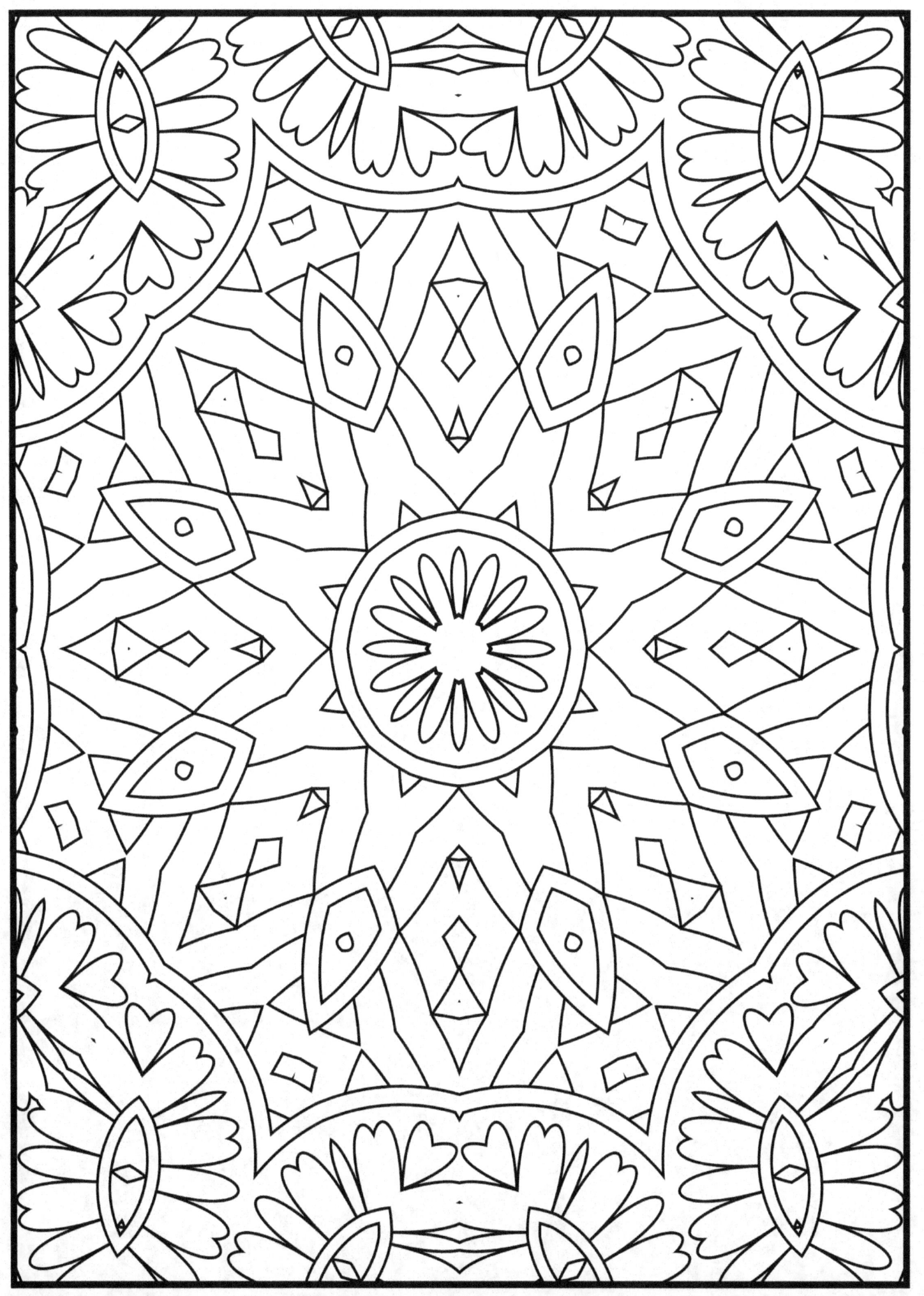

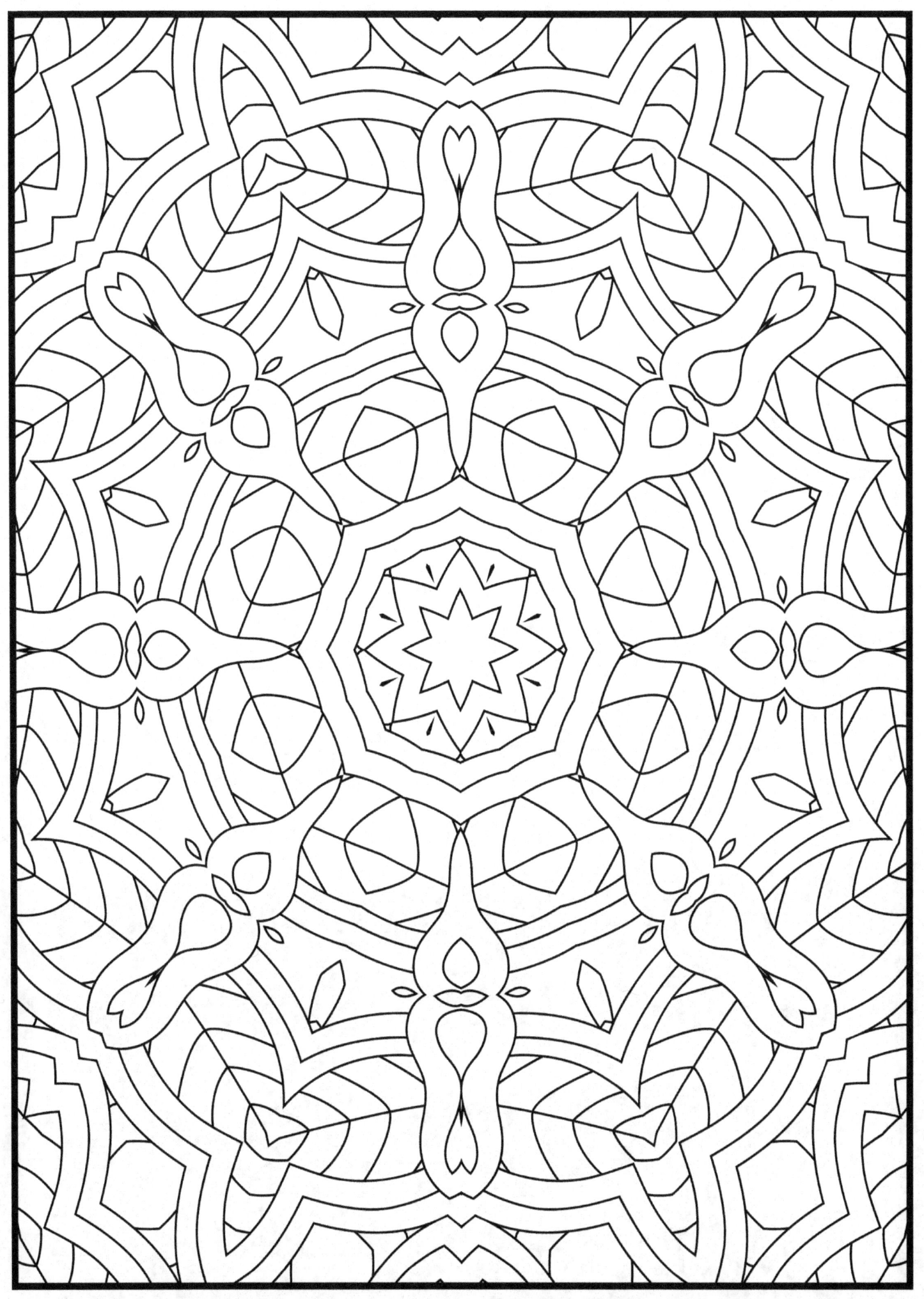

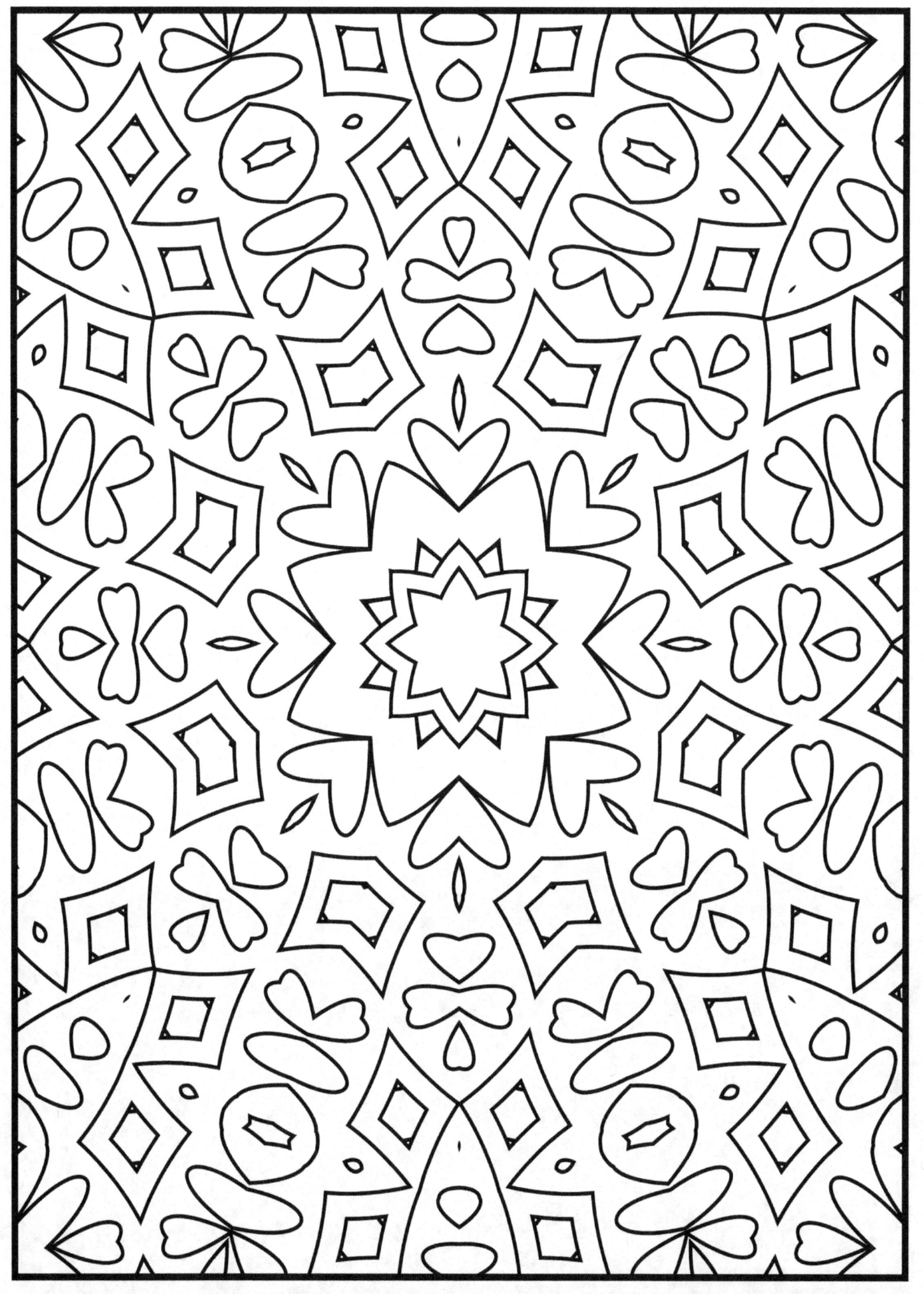

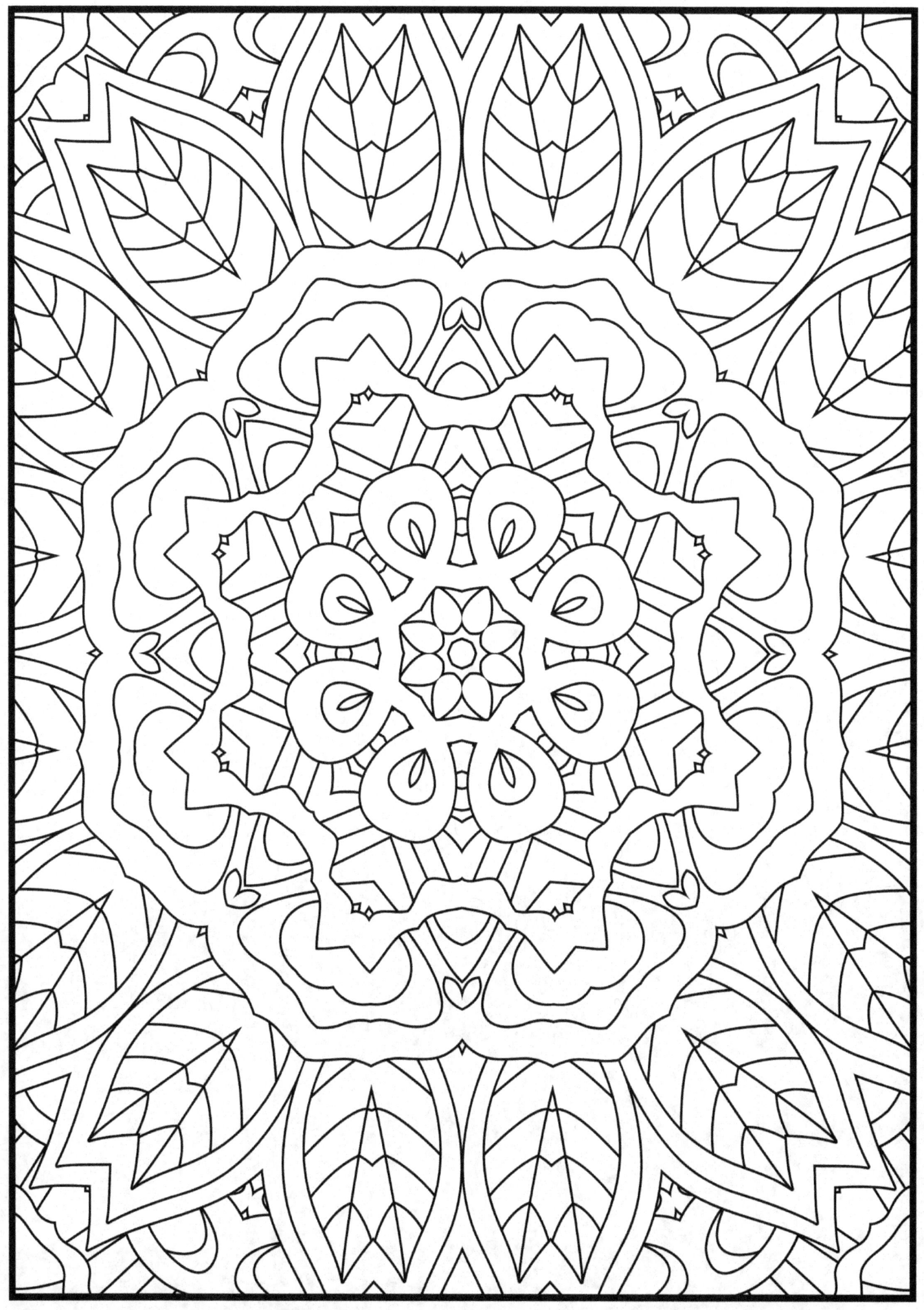

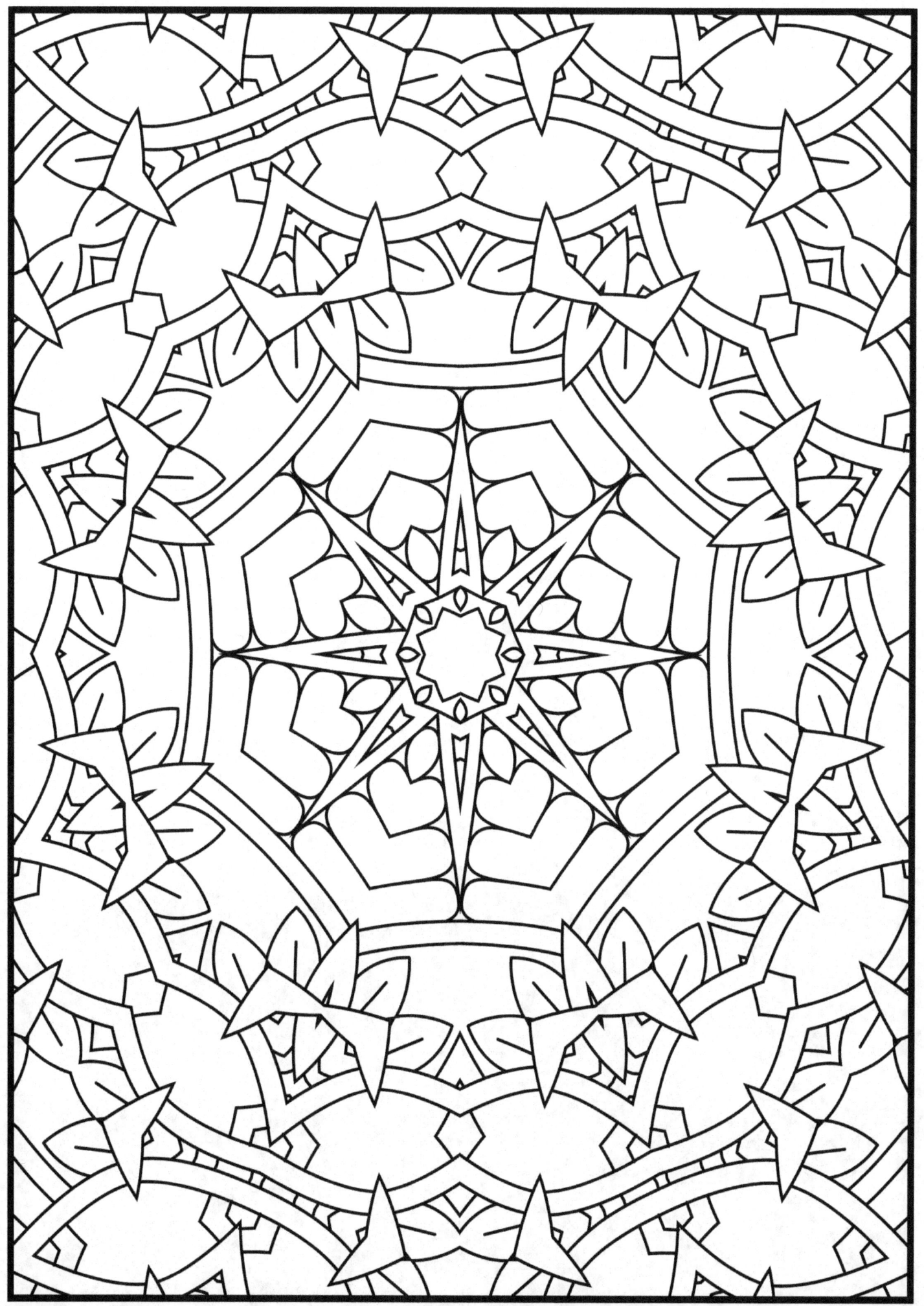

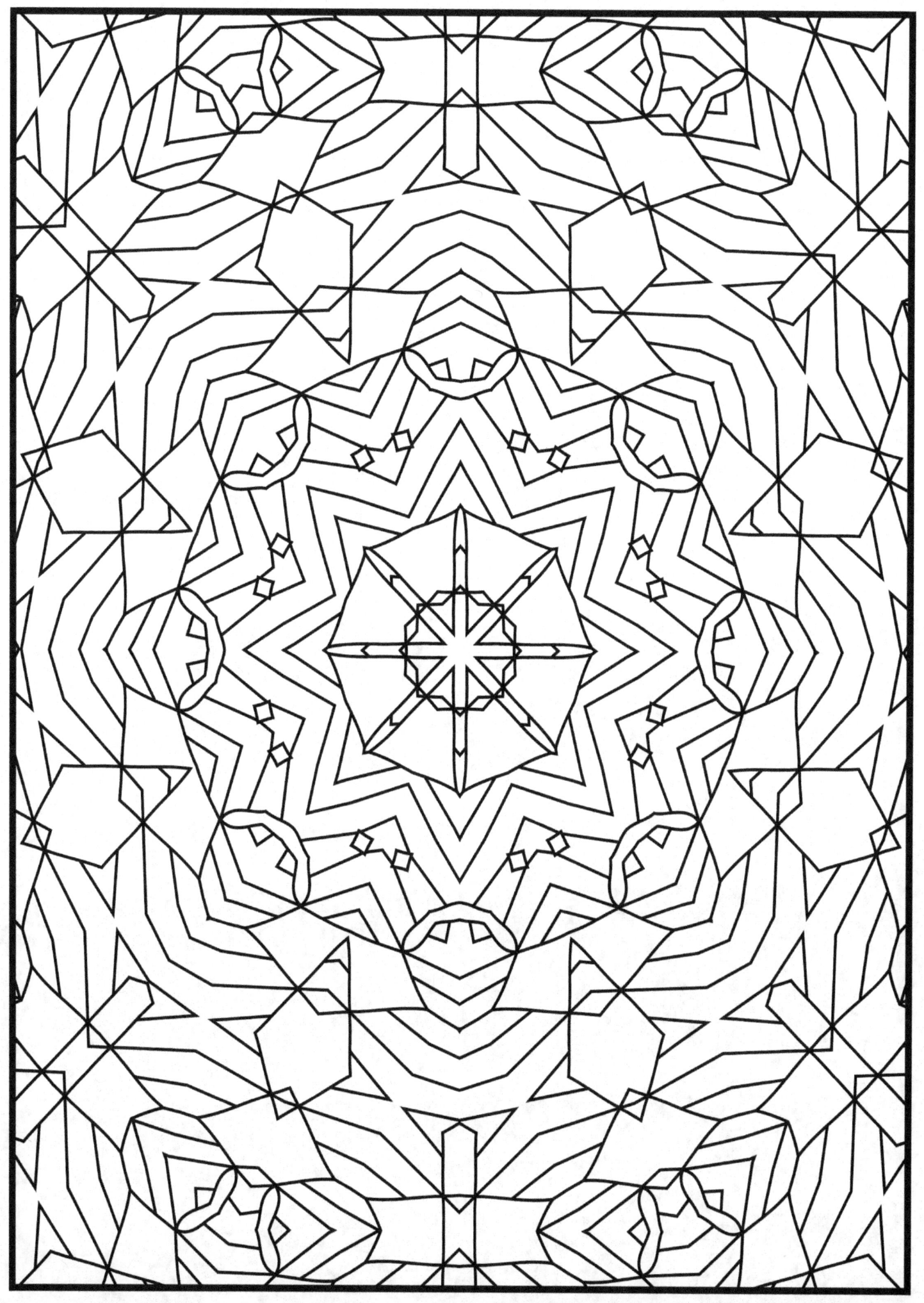

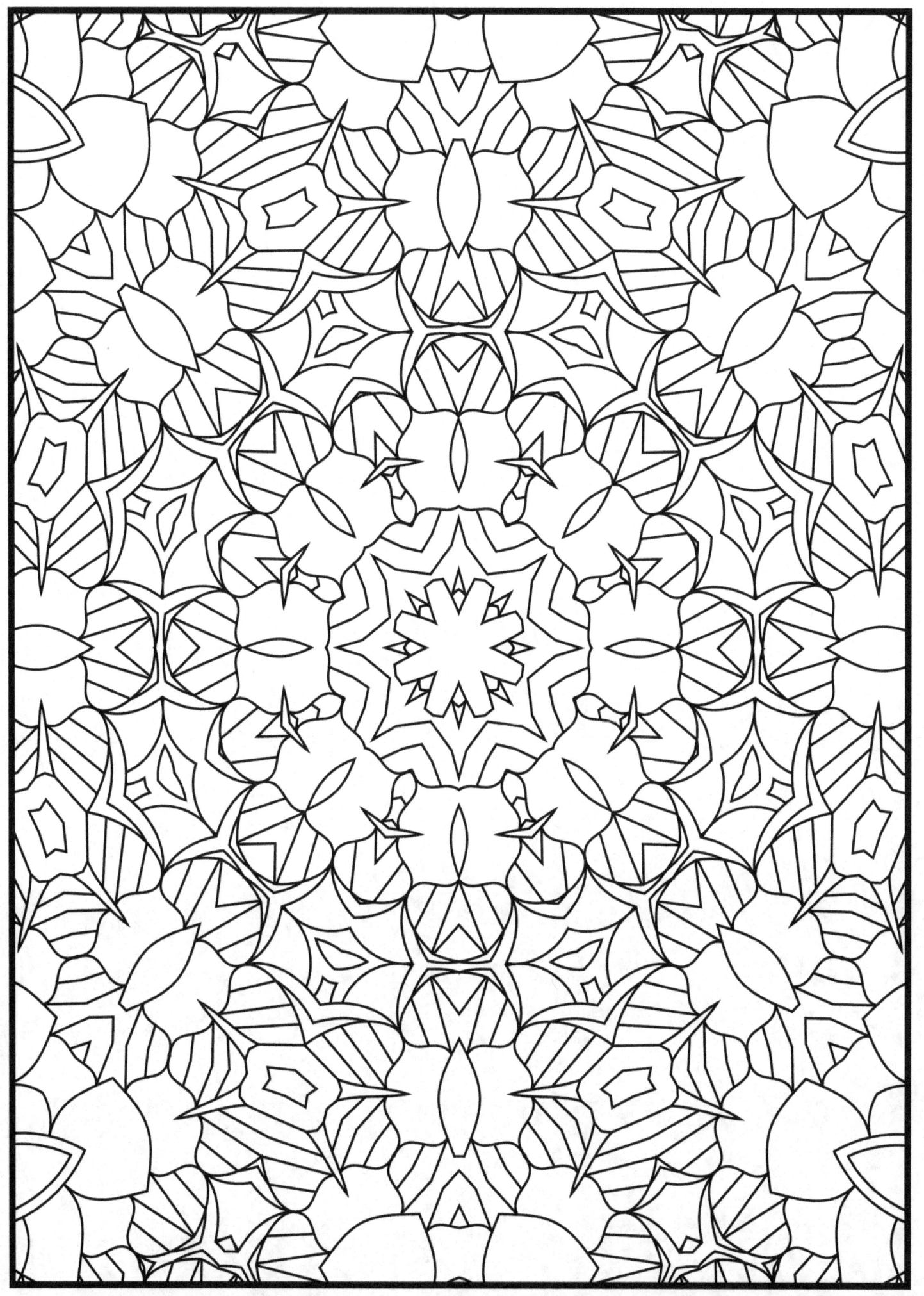

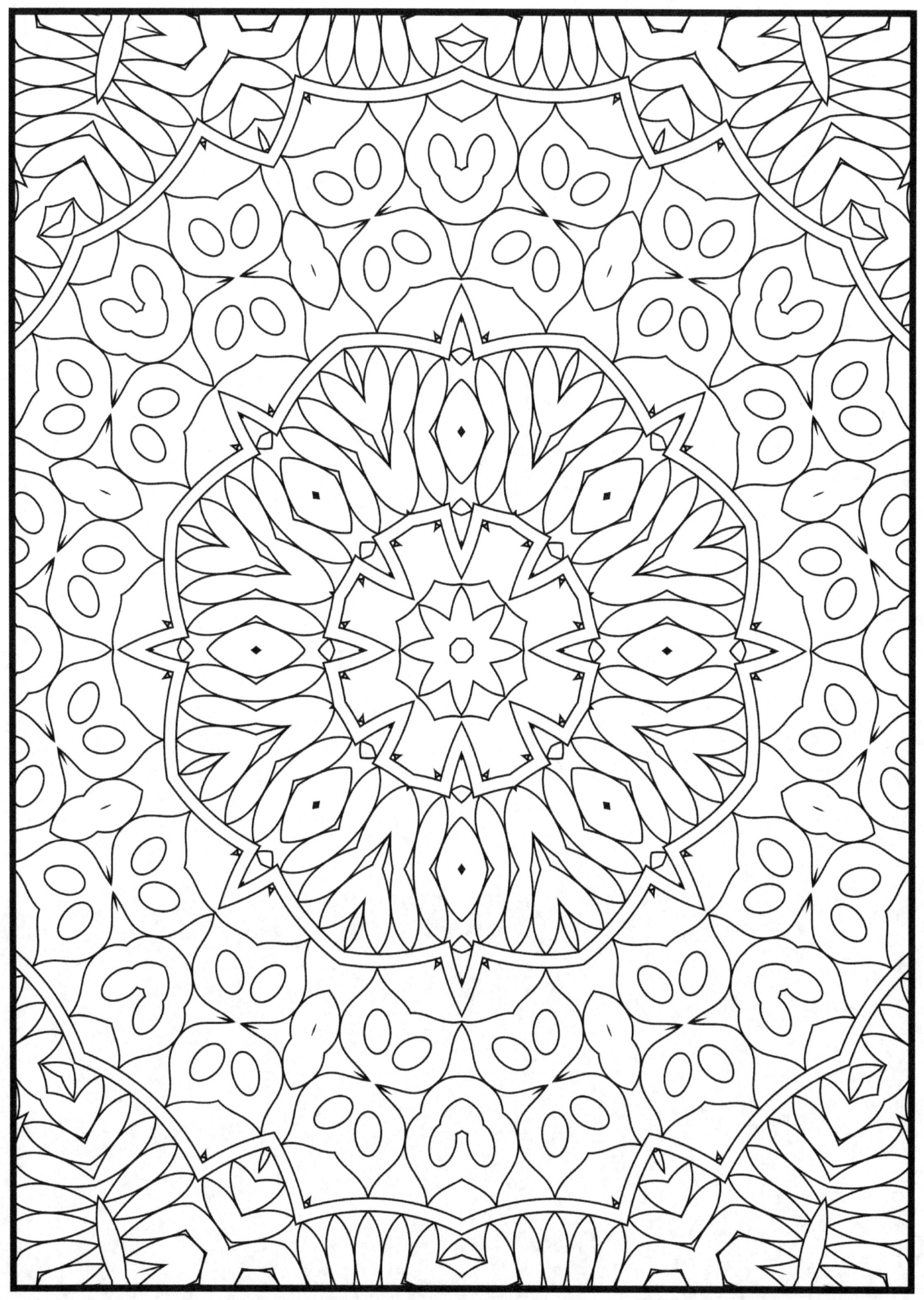

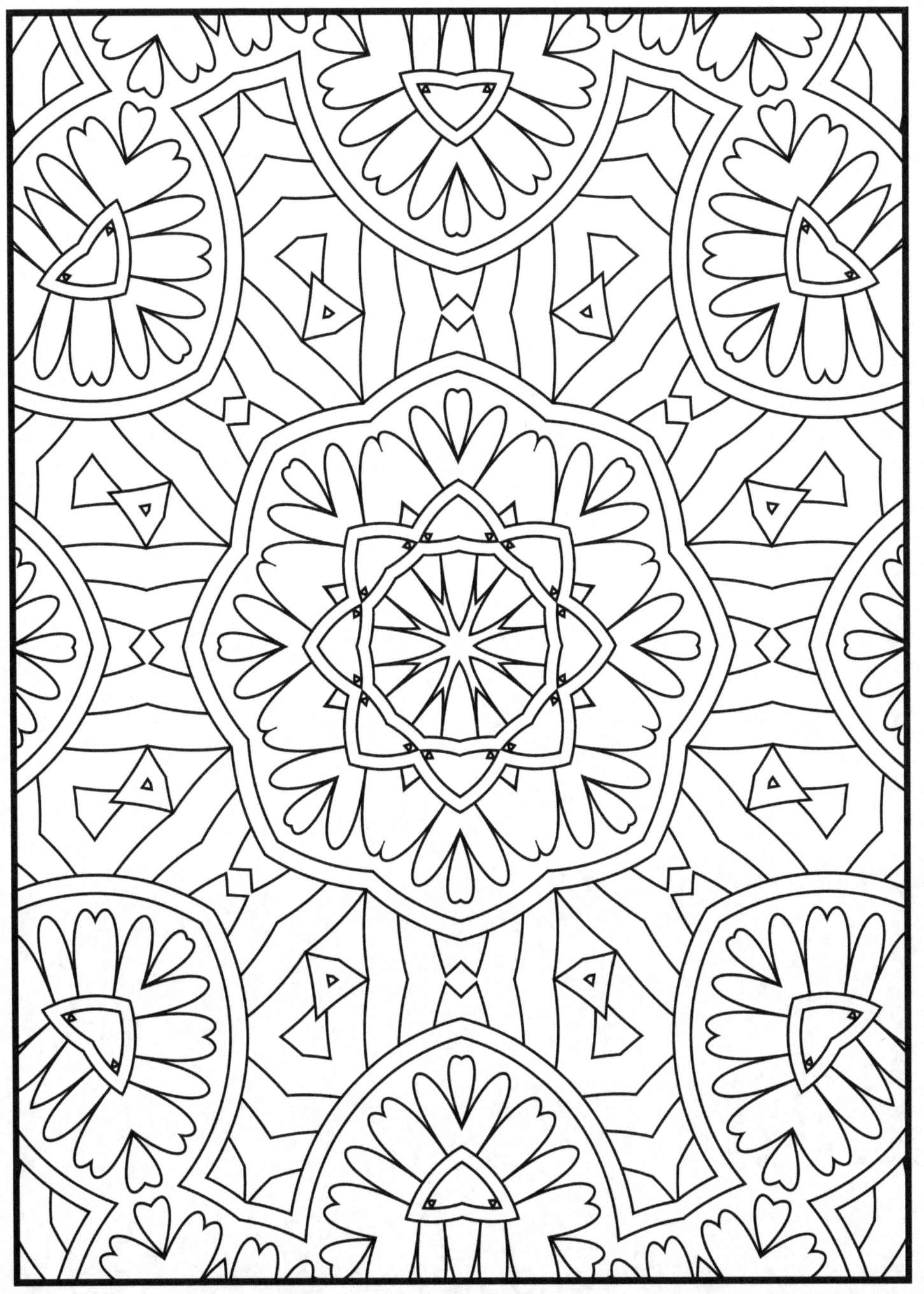

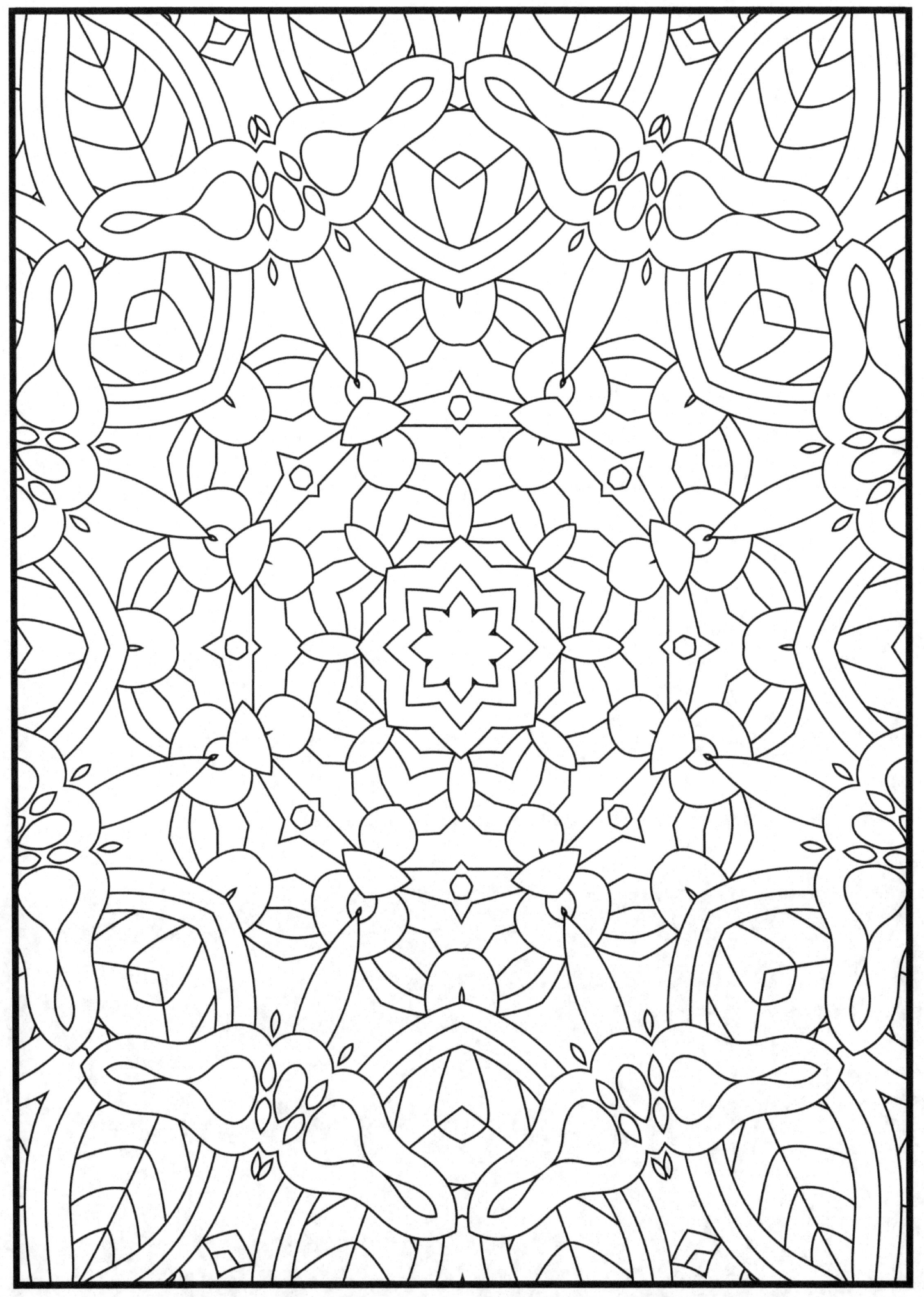

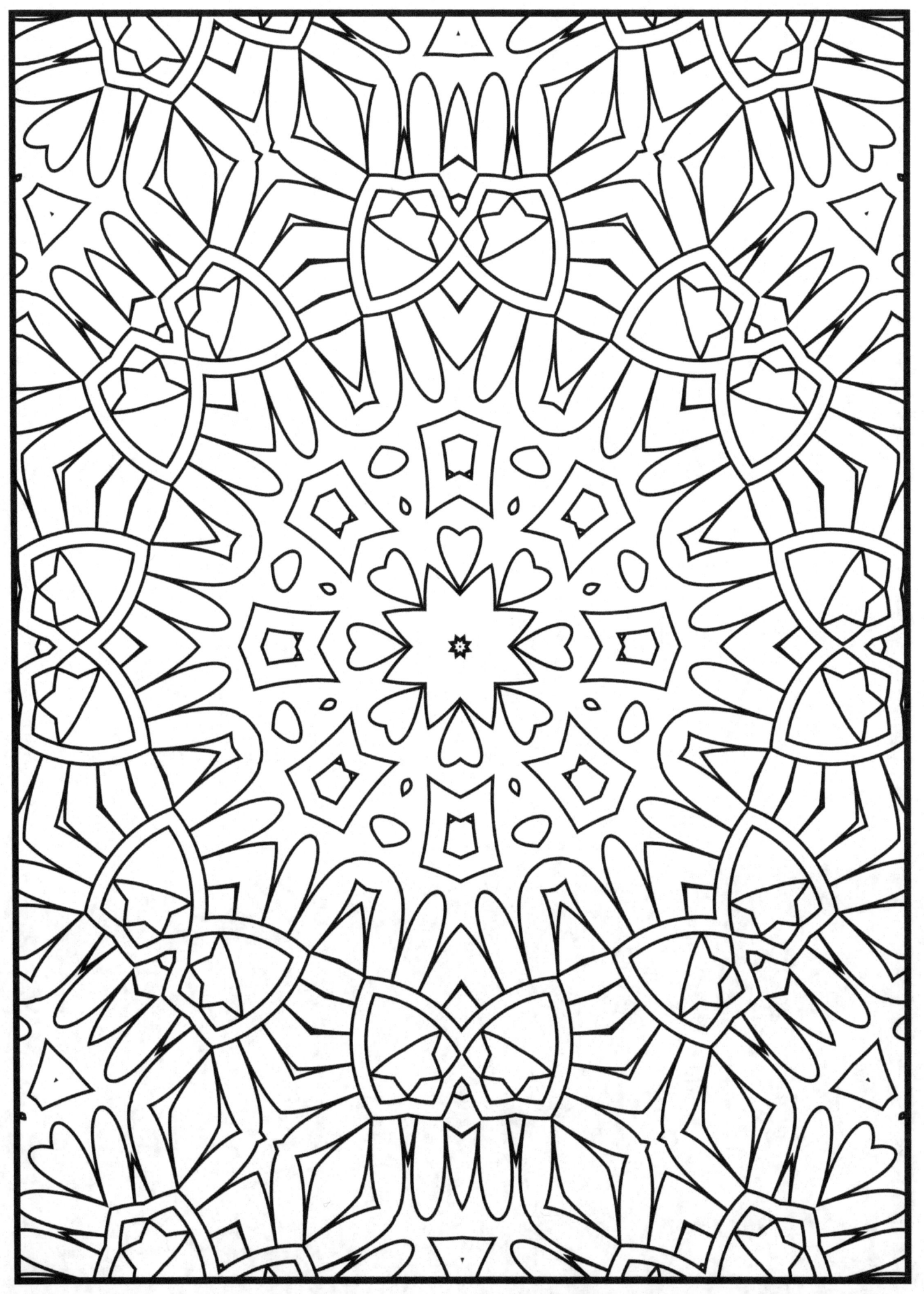

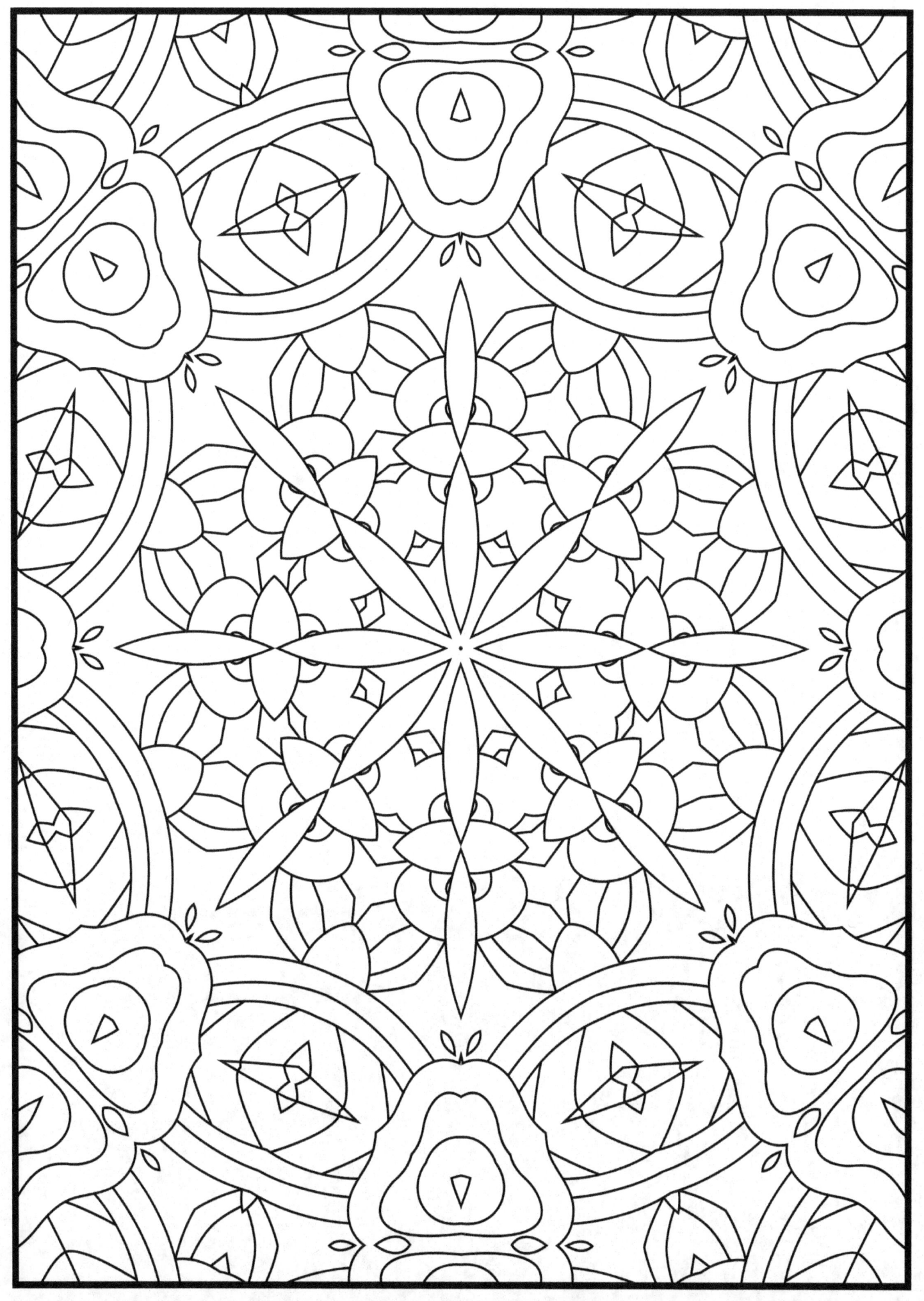

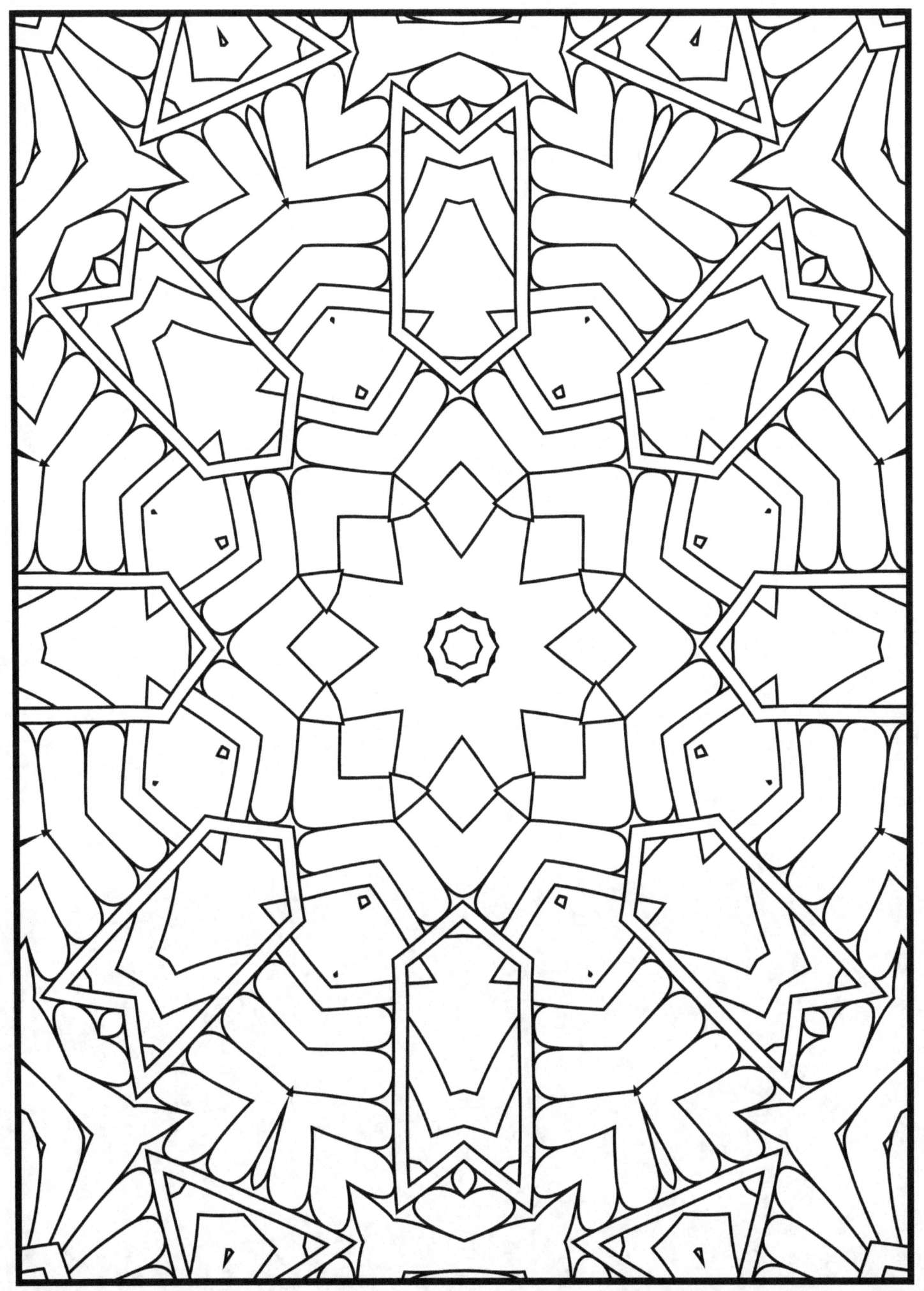

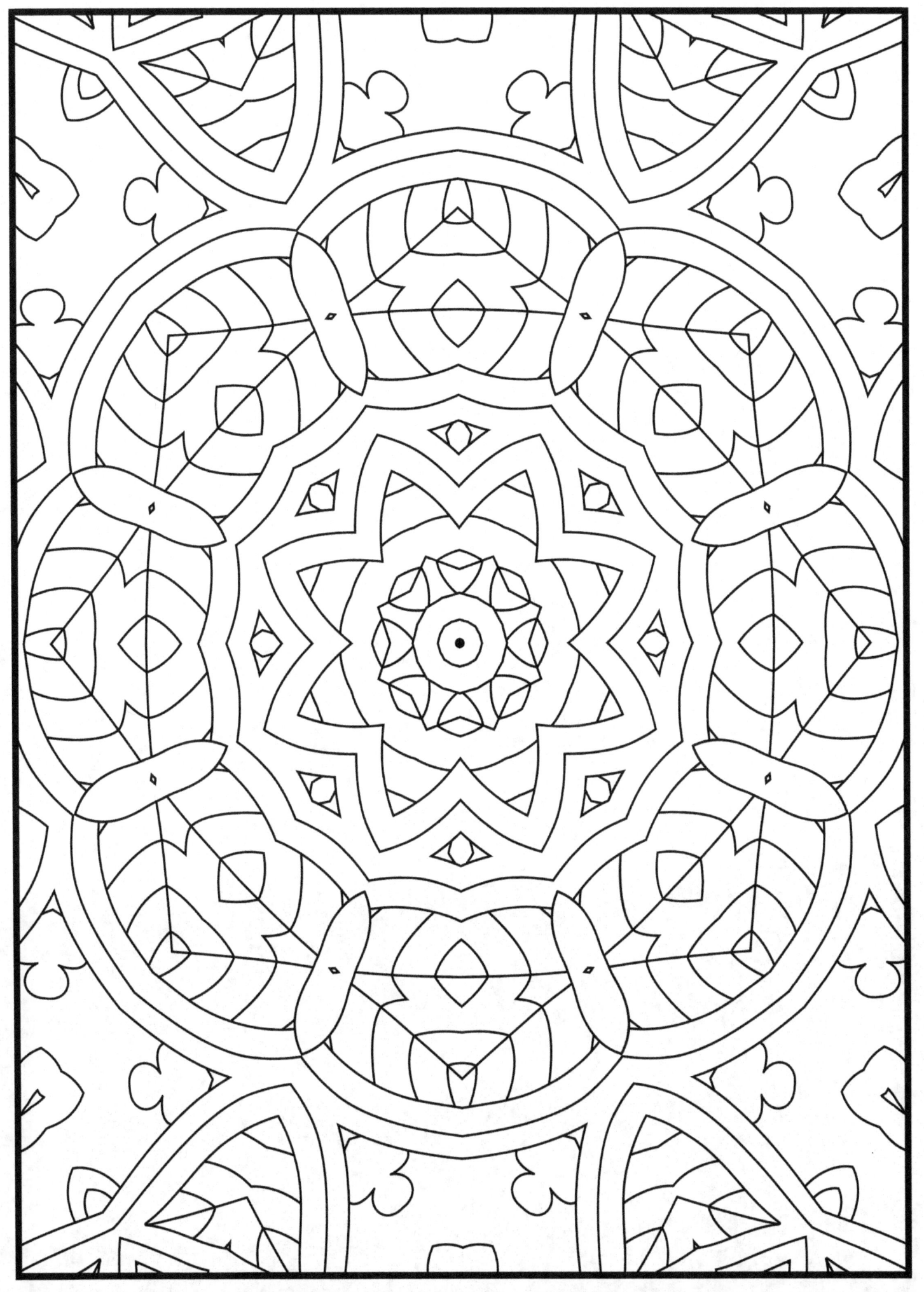

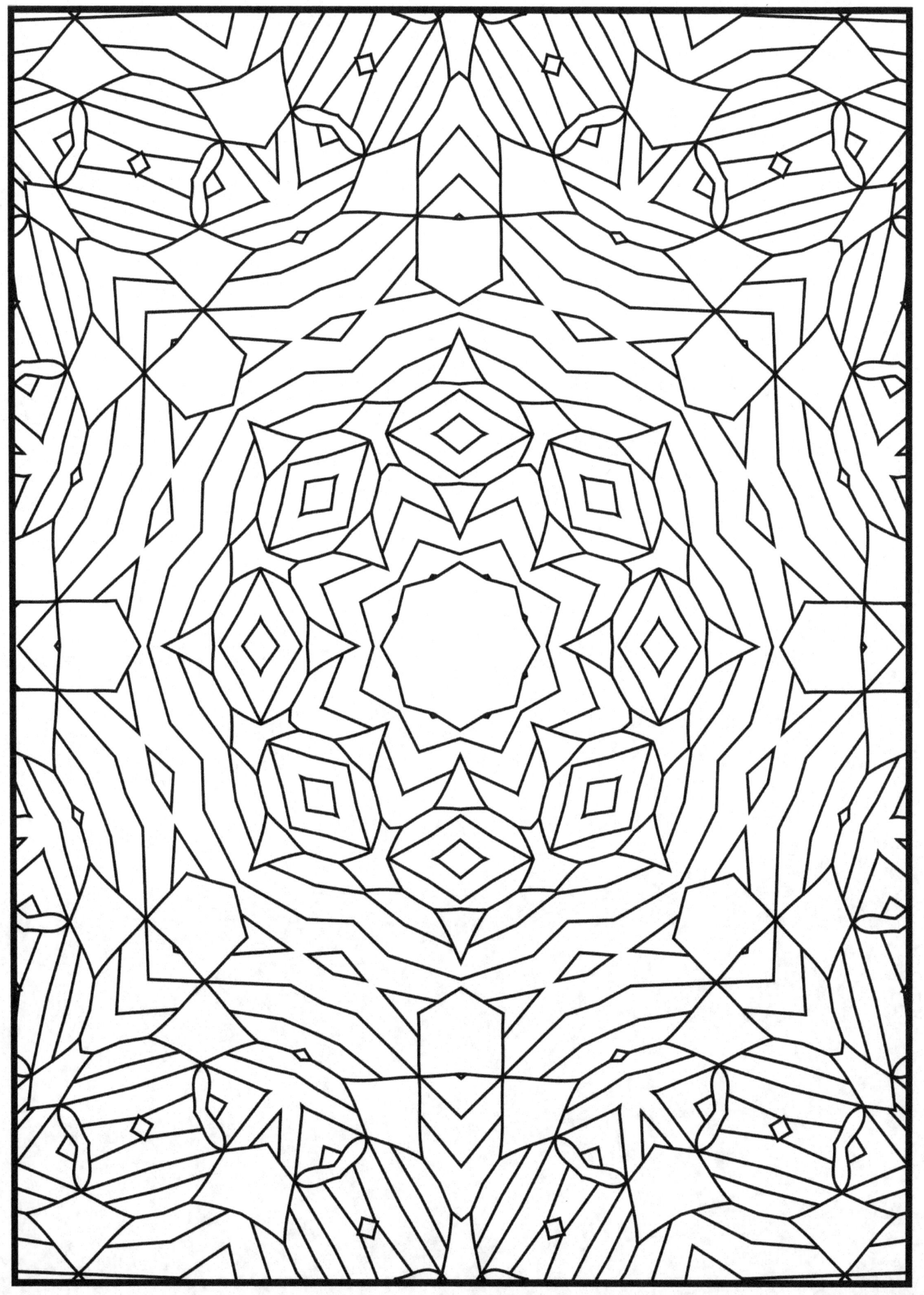

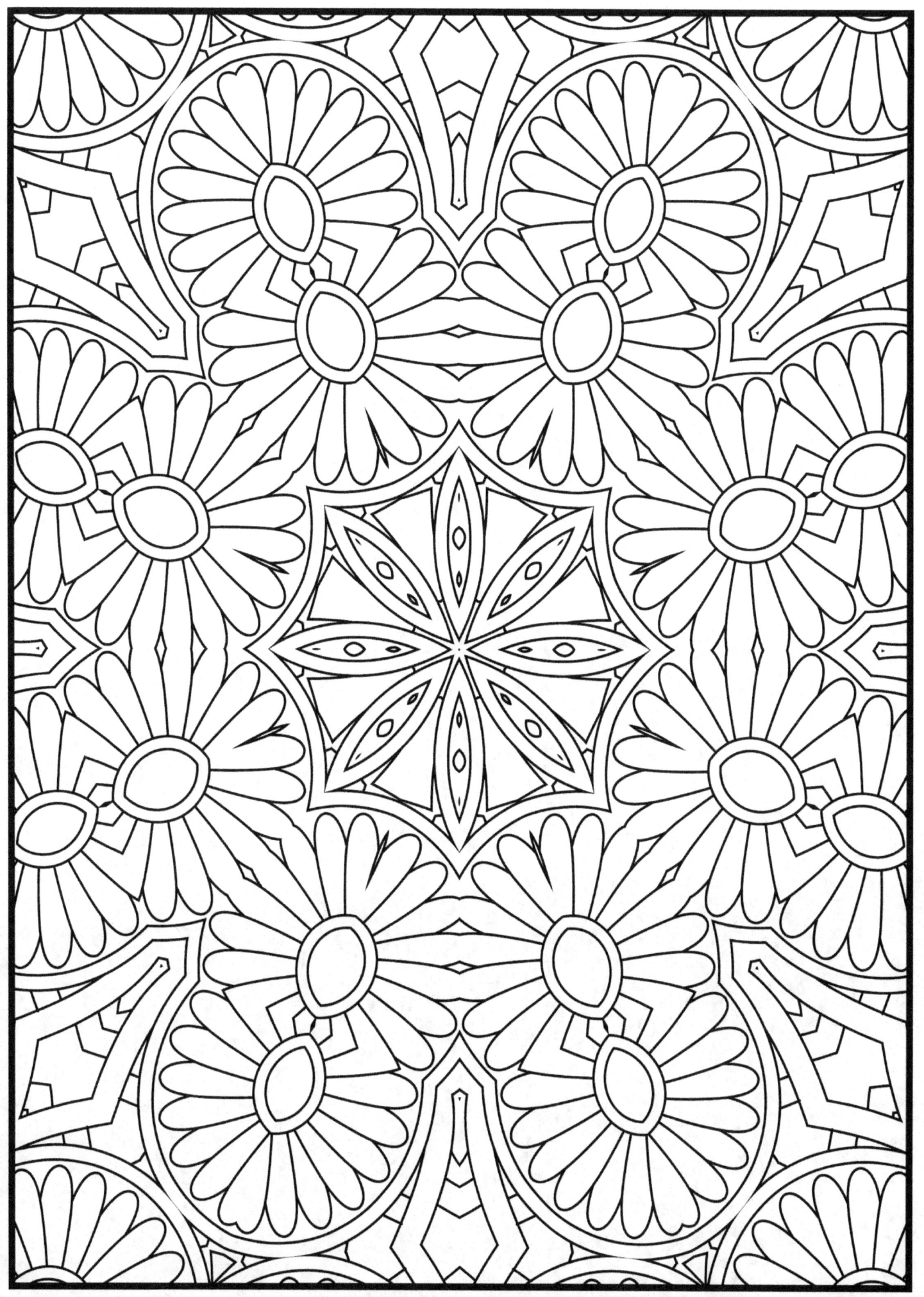

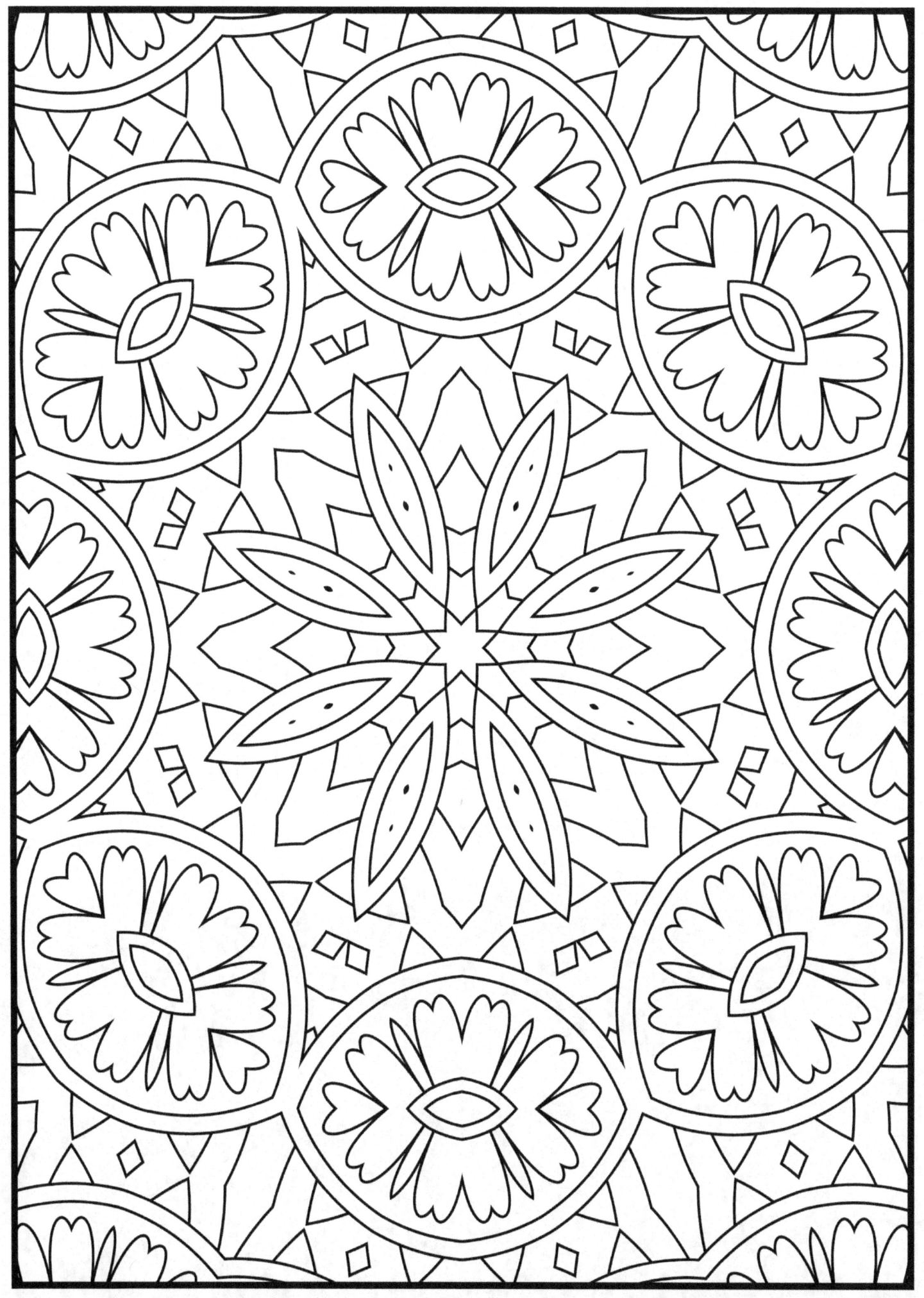

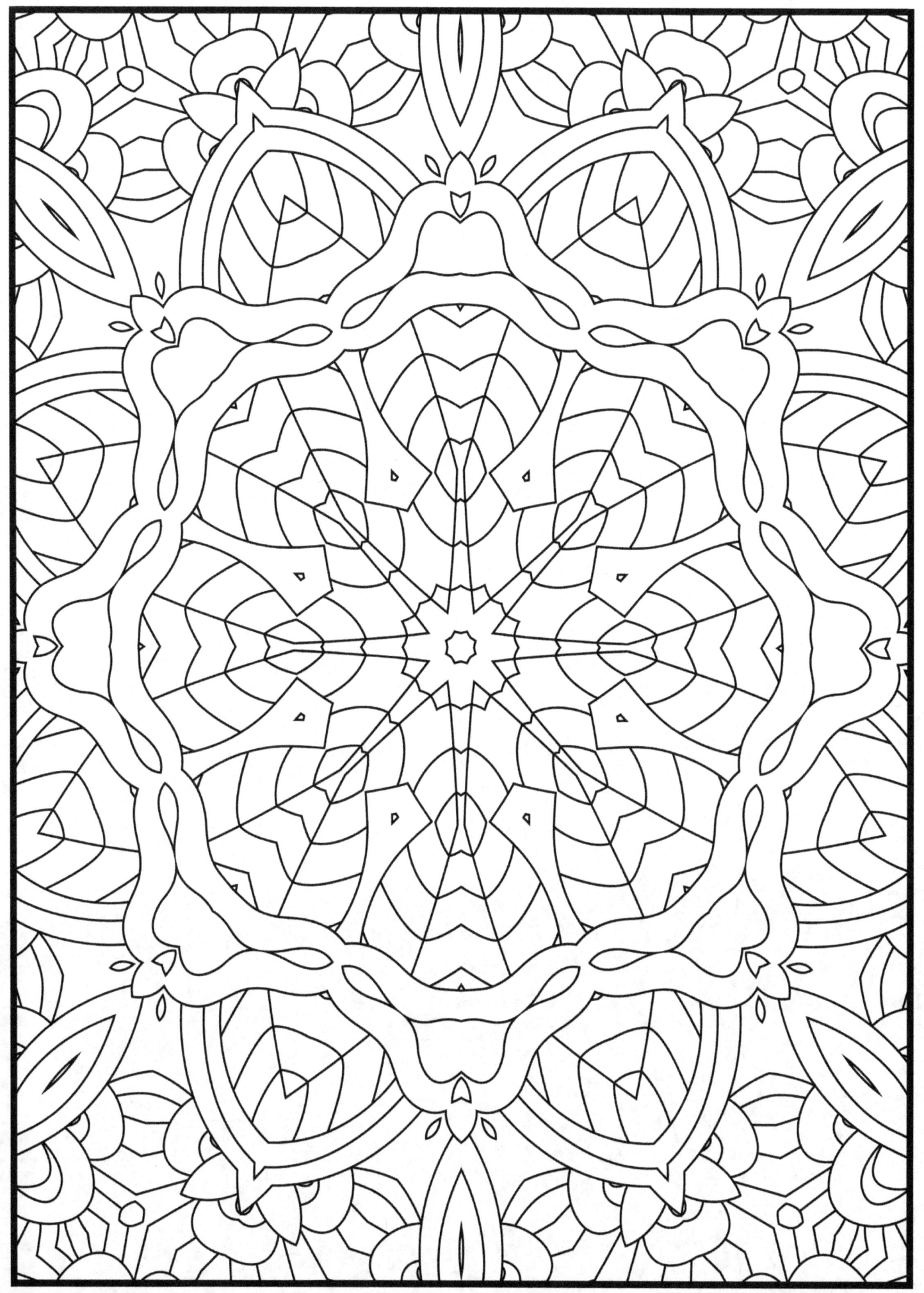

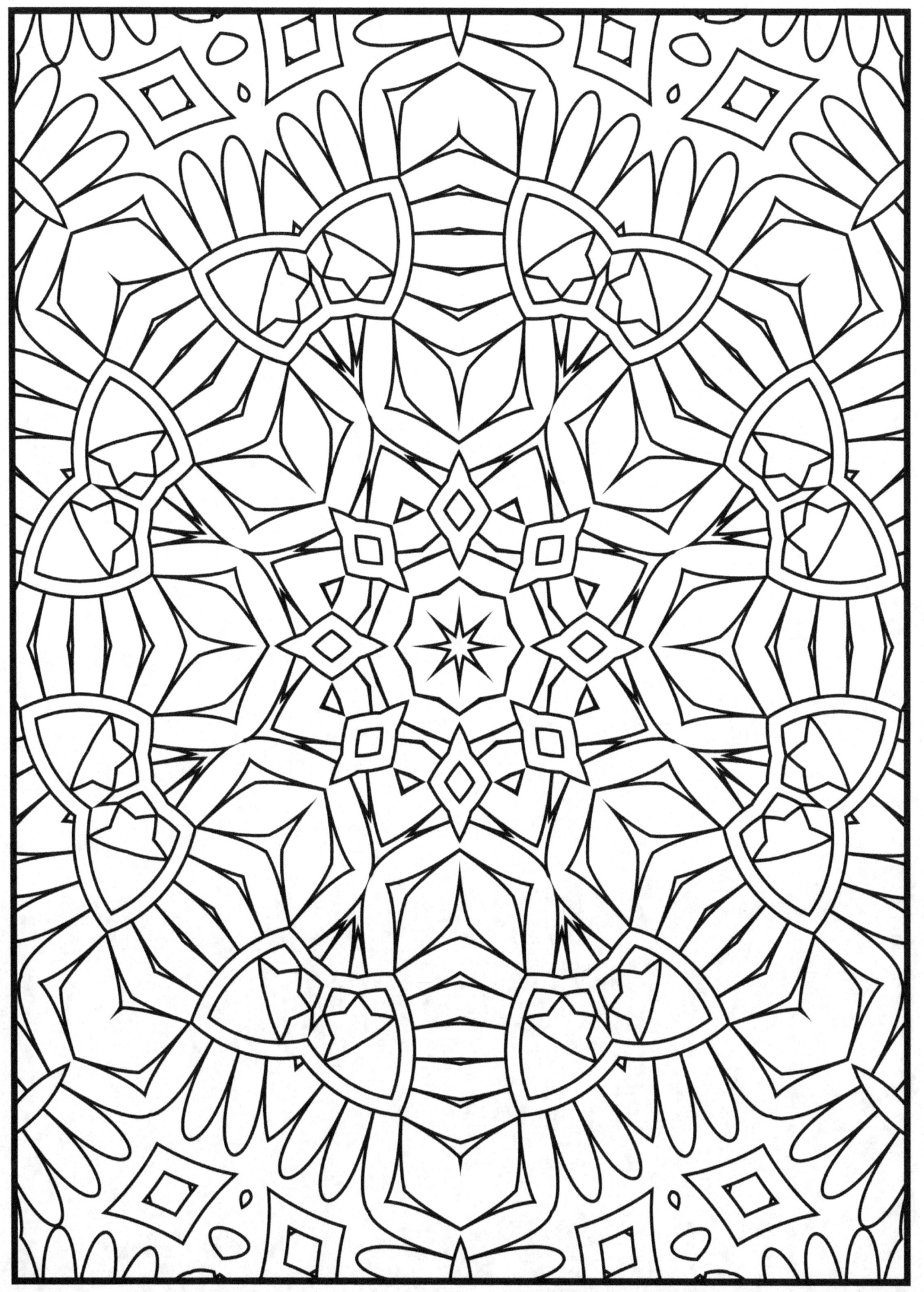

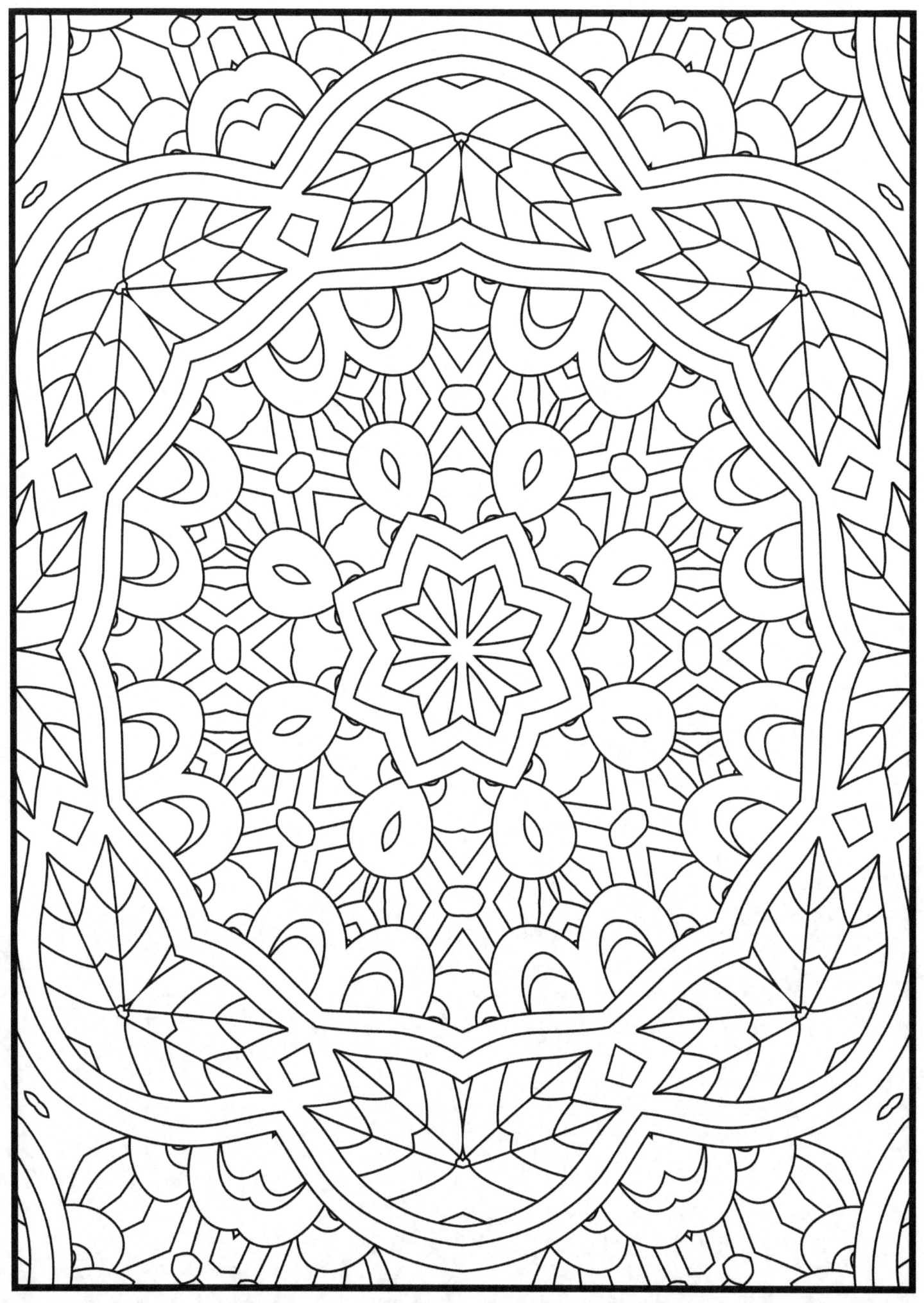

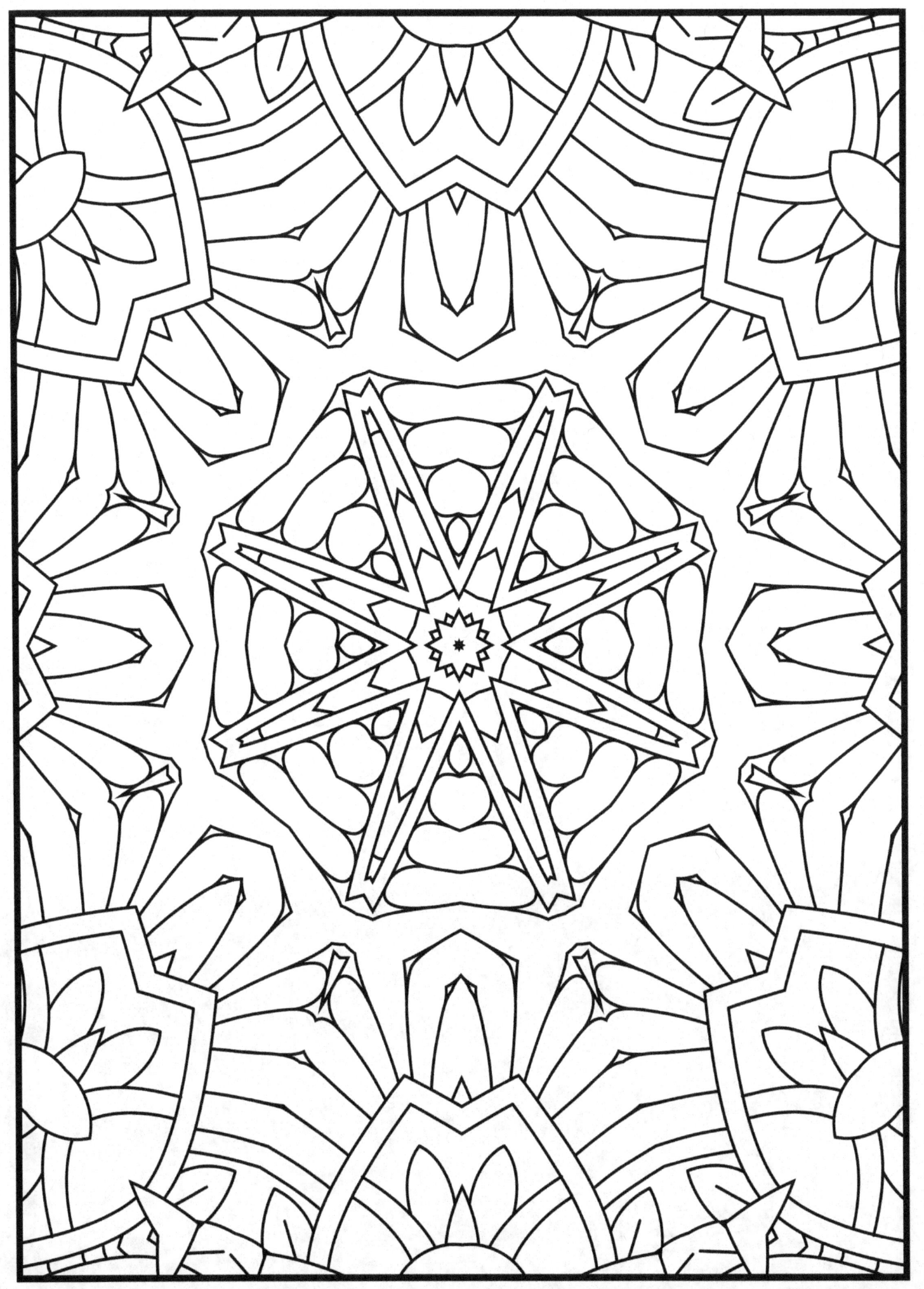

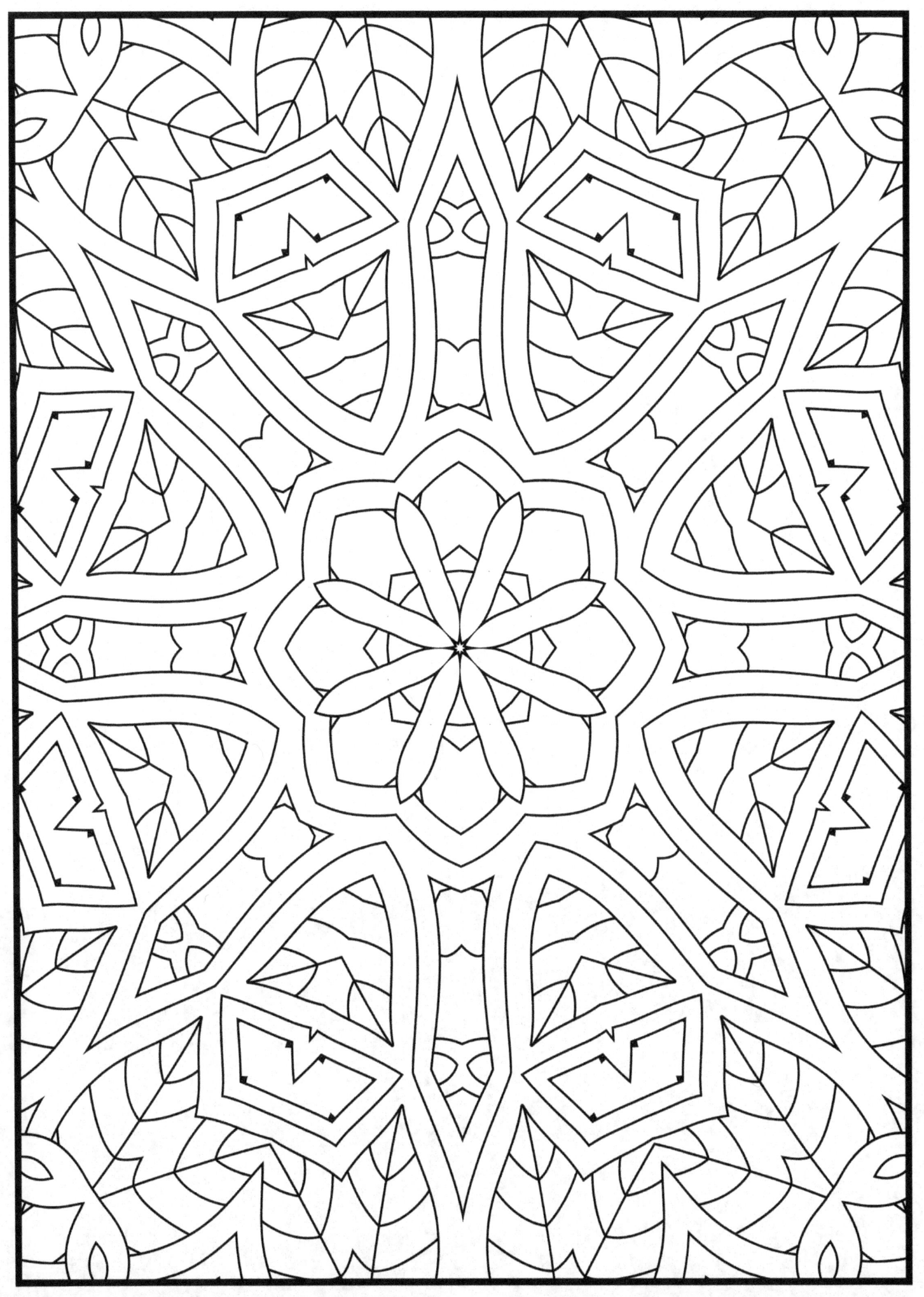

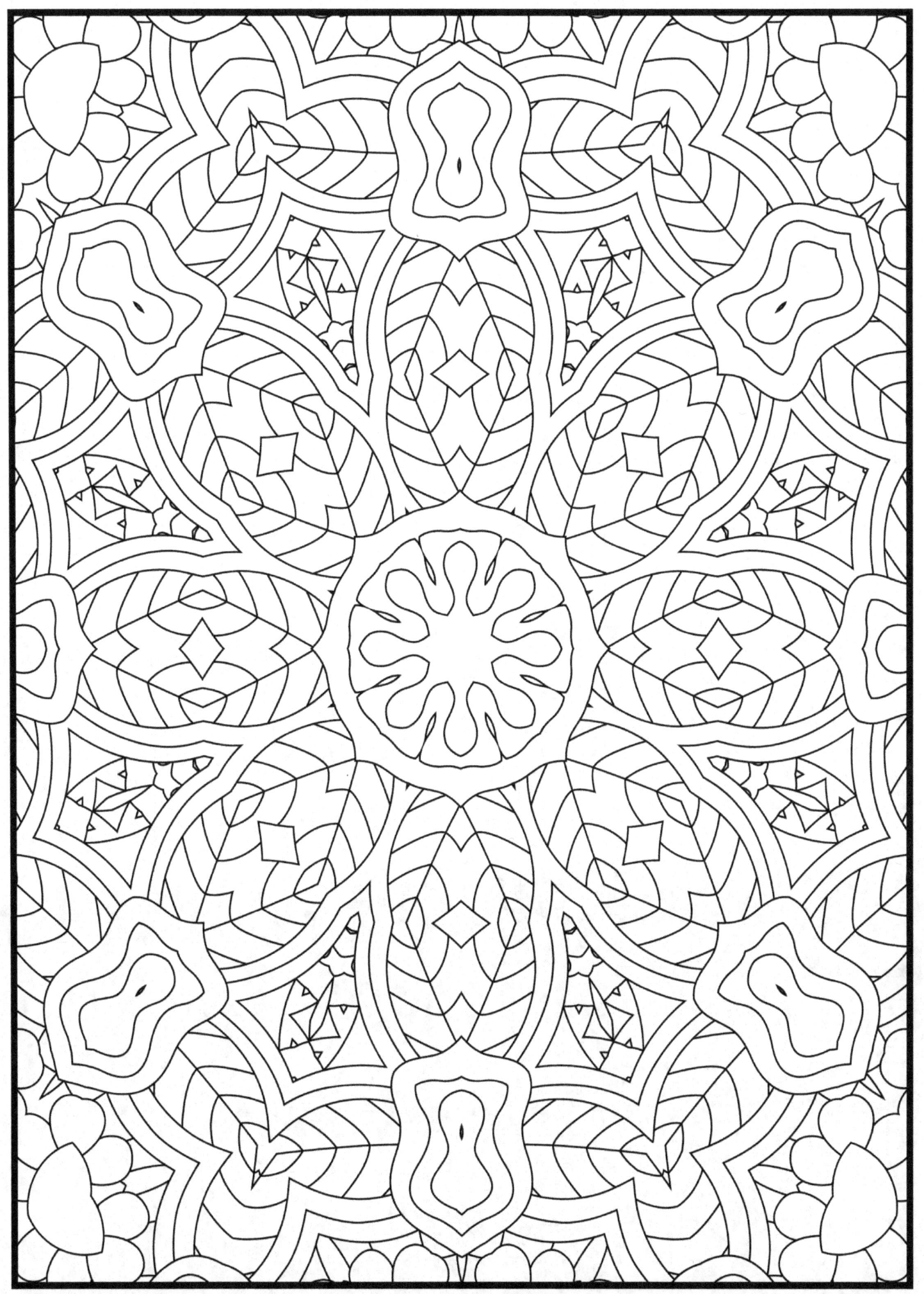